Zimbabwe's Cultural Heritage

Pathisa Nyathi

'amaBooks

ISBN 0-7974-2897-6

Published by 'amaBooks
P.O. Box AC1066, Ascot, Bulawayo
email: amabooks@gatorzw.co.uk

Cover art: Dumisani Ndlovu
(dumiearts@yahoo.com)

'amaBooks would like to express their thanks to the Zimbabwe Culture
Fund Trust for making this publication possible.

Pathisa Nyathi was born in Sankonjana, Kezi, in 1951. He was a teacher, lecturer and head teacher before becoming an Education Officer in 1996. Recently retired from being the Deputy Provincial Education Director for Matabeleland North, he is a published poet, playwright, historian and biographer. He is a columnist for the *Sunday News*, *Umthunywa*, *The Sunday Mirror* and *Sky Host*, as well as being Vice Chair of the Zimbabwe Academic and Non-Fiction Authors Association and a Board Member for a number of organizations.

Previous publications by Pathisa Nyathi

Igugu likaMthwakazi, Imbali yamaNdebele, 1820-1893, Mambo
Press, Gweru, 1994

Uchuku Olungelandiswe Imbai Yama Ndebele 1893-1896, Mambo
Press, Gweru, 1995

In Search of Freedom – Masotsha Ndlovu, Longman, Harare, 1998

Madoda Lolani Incukuthu, Mambo Press, Gweru, 1999

Lawo Magagu: Material Culture of the AmaNdebele, Reach Out,
Pietermaritzburg, 2000

Izibongo Lezangelo ZamaNdebele kaMzilikazi, Reach Out,
Pietermaritzburg, 2000

Alvord Mabena, The Man and His Roots, Priority Projects, Harare,
2000

Traditional Ceremonies of AmaNdebele, Mambo Press, Gweru, 2001

Contents

Introduction

Zimbabwe's Cultural Heritage is a collection of pieces on the culture of the Ndebele, Xhosa, Tonga, Shona, Kalanga, Nambiya and Venda ethnic groups in Zimbabwe. A brief historical background is given for each group, though the emphasis of this book is not on the histories of groups, but on their cultural practices.

Many of the pieces are adaptations of articles that appeared in the *Sunday News* of Bulawayo. In the early days of the author's work with the newspaper, extensive use was made of published sources. However, over the years this changed. This came about as a realization that what is published is already preserved and, therefore, priority must be given to capturing the fading memories of the elders. Scores of people have been interviewed for the material in this book. It is to them that we owe this collection. Sadly, some of them have since died, but their contributions continue to live on in these pages.

Zimbabwe's Cultural Heritage was born out of a desire to promote and preserve for posterity our nation's cultural traditions. The Rhodesian State, whose boundaries were spelt out in the 1889 Royal Charter granted to Cecil John Rhodes by Queen Victoria of England, embraced people who hitherto had lived apart. Consequently, the new state was characterised by a kaleidoscopic cultural landscape.

The colonising culture became the dominant culture. The subservient cultures began to incorporate elements from the ruling culture and underwent fundamental changes.

Despite the process of acculturation that ensued, the dominated cultures have some of their elements surviving to this day. This book seeks to capture the cultural practices before western culture impacted on them. Where some aspects of the indigenous culture have undergone change, this book seeks to highlight those changes and to explain the forces that have been at work.

The new Zimbabwean State has a variety of cultures, but it has inherited a legacy of a domineering culture. Most people would see merit in a nation that is characterised by an awareness and appreciation of the cultures of all of its groups.

In Zimbabwe today, there are common unifying elements of African culture. For example, the substance of religion is common to all African peoples. None of them communicated directly with God. Instead, they did so through a hierarchy of departed ancestors. Propitiation of the departed ancestors so that they intercede with God on behalf of their living progeny places a two way communication system at the heart of African religion.

All the African peoples in Zimbabwe who apparently belonged to the Bantu race did not espouse separation of powers in their philosophy of governance. Religious power, political power, judicial power and, indeed, other forms of power tended to be fused in the same individual. Among the Shona there was some separation of the religious and political authorities. The two worked together and religious authority kept political authority in check. Thus political excesses were kept under control.

It is appropriate to give some indication as to how society was organized. The basic unit was the extended family. This was the working unit on a day to day basis. Members of the family worked together in all aspects of life. The males were the heads of families.

A group of families that shared the same totem constituted a clan. In general terms a totem related to some natural thing, for example an animal, bird or plant. A totemic animal was revered and members bearing a particular totem did not eat their totemic animal. Totems defined marital boundaries. In most cases there were no intra-totemic marriages.

Over a period of time, clans combined to constitute an ethnic group. This could also be referred to as a tribe. Such a group shared a common history, the same traditions and world view. They would also fall under the same political authority.

This book recognises the different historical paths followed by each ethnic group. For convenience and in recognition of the historical realities, the cultural heritage of each group has been given separately. It is acknowledged that not all ethnic groups have been covered. For example, the Sotho/Birwa of Matabeleland South, the Hlengwe and Shangane of Masvingo have not been included in this first volume. Nor has western culture been considered.

It is the author's hope that the project will expand and embrace the remaining cultural groups. It is also hoped that a deeper examination will be made of the cultural groups already included in this volume.

The book is intended for all those who are interested in the cultural practices of their own ancestors and the ancestors of others. Further, the various traditional cultural practices help to throw some light on current happenings. Why would a relation of a deceased woman dump her corpse on the doorstep of her husband? Why would the Tonga be more amenable to democratic practice?

The present, sculptured on the anvil of the past, fashions the future. We need to understand our past in order to move with confidence into the future.

One distinct characteristic of the book is the use of words, phrases and expressions in indigenous languages. This was a deliberate strategy to capture the language that was contemporary to the times when the various cultural practices were in vogue. Translations of these names and phrases are given, or their meaning understood by their context. Where people or places have multiple names, a single version is used after the initial occurrence. A glossary is given at the end of the book for some common words.

The author would like to thank Dr Godfrey Tabona Ncube of Midlands State University for his contribution to this book.

THE NDEBELE

The Ndebele of Zimbabwe constituted themselves into a migrant kingdom around 1821. The original Nguni group came out of the Zulu, Ndwandwe, Mthethwa and Swazi States. Their King was Mzilikazi Khumalo, a son of Matshobana. His mother was probably Cikose Ndiweni. The Ndebele were the last to leave Zululand. Parties led by Zwangendaba Jele, Sotshangane Nxumalo, Ngwana Masseko and Nqaba had gone ahead of the Ndebele.

The general cataclysmic dispersal of the people from the south-eastern seaboard of South Africa is referred to as *Mfecane*. Generally, there are two theories that are used to explain this great scattering. The first theory is that King Tshaka of the Zulu was behind it all. His imperial and military consolidations were the cause of great suffering and hence the dispersal to avoid his conquering campaigns. As a result, there was a general depopulation of the interior. This theory is in line with apartheid philosophy – whites moving into the area did not take away land from the blacks.

The second theory attributes the great scattering to economic activities at the Cape and also in the Delagoa Bay (Maputo) area of Mozambique. Industrial activities in the Cape needed labour that was obtained from the interior. The hunt for labour put pressure on the people to the north-east of the Cape. Another source of pressure was the slaving activity taking place in the Delagoa area. African groups inland began to compete to control the trade routes to the sea. Slave hunters were at work causing strife in the whole area. While it is true that nations in the general area did turn on each other, the underlying causes were the pressure to service the growing industries and the slave trading on the Mozambique coast

Leading a group of no more than 500, Mzilikazi led his people over the Drakensberg Mountains, Izintaba zoKhahlamba. In order to beef up his nascent kingdom, he incorporated Sotho/Tswana and Pedi people he encountered in the Transvaal (now the Gauteng, Limpopo and Mpumalanga Provinces).

King Mzilikazi established three settlements south of the Limpopo River. The first, from 1822 to 1827, was on the Vaal River, uLikhwa. The second, from 1827 to 1832, was where present day Pretoria is located. The third and final one was in the Marico Valley in Western Transvaal.

It was Griqua raids on the Ndebele - in search of cattle – that forced King Mzilikazi and his people to consider moving on. There were also raids from the Zulu once Dingane became king in 1828. However, the decisive factor was an attack, in 1837, by the Boers under Andries Hendrick Potgieter and Sarel Cilliers. The King split his people into two groups that became separated from each other for two years.

The Ndebele established a final home in south-western Zimbabwe, where they found the Rozvi State already weakened by Queen Nyamazana's Swazi, who had separated from Zwangendaba's group on its way to the north.

King Mzilikazi reunited the two sections of his people and incorporated indigenous groups into his new state. Queen Nyamazana Dlamini, who had established a state called Mthwakazi, was married to King Mzilikazi. By means of that marriage arrangement, King Mzilikazi took over the State of Mthwakazi and maintained its name. The king died in 1868 and was succeeded by his son Lobengula after a bloody civil war. Colonial machinations led to the demise of the State of Mthwakazi.

Mthwakazi was attacked. Lobengula fled north after ordering Bulawayo (his last capital where present day Bulawayo stands) burnt. It was all over. Colonial rule took root. The Ndebele were evicted from their former homes. Two reserves were set aside for their occupation – namely Shangani (now Nkayi and Lupane) and Gwayi (Tsholotsho).

In terms of culture, the Ndebele are closest to the Zulu and other Nguni groups of South Africa. Ndebele society today consists of the original Nguni group that came out of Zululand, the Sotho/Tswana incorporates and the Shona – Kalanga – Rozvi peoples who were indigenous to Zimbabwe. Inevitably, the original Ndebele culture has undergone changes, though, essentially, it is still close to Zulu culture.

Face to face with the spirit of Africa

I looked at the sun, which was about to perform its daily ritual of departure. This meant the dual ceremony was about to start. It was dual because my aunt and her daughter were being 'brought home' simultaneously. I had looked forward to this day because I had not witnessed *umbuyiso* before.

A short energetic man clapped his hands to draw our attention. Suddenly, people wore sad faces and trudged towards my father, who was standing, with a characteristic stoop, in front of the kitchen hut. He was the chief priest cum master of ceremonies. Relatives gathered around my father for a briefing on how the double ceremony was going to be conducted. My father opened up the debate to the relatives. No insurmountable hitches were encountered. It was agreed that my aunt would be brought home first, her daughter soon after.

The people present spoke in hushed tones, in deference to the people whose souls were being brought home. Ndebele religious philosophy posits that human beings have a spiritual component that lives on beyond the grave. This spirit, separated from the body, wanders into the unfathomable abyss of the universe. It wanders in solitude until it is brought back home to take care of its earthly progeny.

Just when we all thought everything was in place, one woman brought to our attention the fact that my aunt's daughter had been buried in Bulawayo, and that soil from her grave had been brought along. A momentary uneasy silence was broken by a piercing dry cough from an old man. The man suggested a ritual burial of the soil prior to conducting the bringing home ceremonies.

I heard a few loud sighs of relief and observed several heads nodding in agreement. At that point, we all went to the back of the homestead where my aunt was buried. Next to her grave a small hole was dug, and the soil from Bulawayo interred in this ritual grave. The short ceremony was marked by the solemnity that is characteristic of a burial.

Once back at the homestead, preparations for the next phase began. We were shown two calabashes containing consecrated beer: one for my aunt and another for my cousin. A she-goat was dragged from the pen. My worst fear came true. The responsibility of holding the jittery goat fell on me. In essence, it meant that I was to bring home the wandering spirit of my aunt and request it to take charge of its children.

My aunt's eldest daughter balanced the calabash with frothing beer on her head and led the way to my aunt's grave. I followed her, struggling to control the wild goat. I mustered all my strength. If the bleating thing bolted it could be misinterpreted as my aunt's spirit refusing to come home. I was not prepared to take responsibility for such a tragedy.

Now the officiating priest, my father, knelt beside the tombstone. Prayerfully, he announced to my aunt's spirit what we were about to do. He beseeched her to come home and take care of her children. As he uttered these words he poured some beer on the grave. He took a small quantity in his mouth, spat it out and then swallowed a small mouthful. Beer was poured over the back of the goat, which I was still holding with all my strength.

Silence descended. The goat, its back wet with beer, tried to pull a trick or two in order to bolt away. No, my aunt's spirit bolting away into the void where it had been wandering along? I held it so tightly that it could only succeed in getting away if it left its horns with me.

Every person present took a sip of the beer in turn. The first sip was spat out and the second swallowed. A little beer should always be left in the calabash. This, my father poured onto the grave.

The joyful return started with me now the centre of attention. In my own hands I held the spirit of my aunt which I led home to her children. The *izinyanga* song, during which my aunt's name was called out, accompanied our triumphal spiritual entry into the homestead. Sweating profusely, I was ordered to stand in front of the sacrificial hut, with the goat still firmly held in my hands. The singing party entered the hut and continued with the singing. Finally, to my relief, the goat was taken away from me to be slaughtered.

A few women with beer calabashes arrived as we prepared to repeat the same procedure for my cousin. These women were met by ululating women of the homestead, who took away the calabashes to a makeshift enclosure.

Meanwhile, another she-goat was taken from the pen. This time I was spared the agony of grappling with a goat. With the two goats cooking in the pots, some men went to the cattle kraal to slaughter the first cow. The second would be slaughtered the next morning. For beef starved urbanites like myself, a memorable feast ensued.

I remembered an energetic schoolgirl from Josiah Chinamano School in Bulawayo who did a project on various Zimbabwean foods. This was during Scholastica. Her map showed beef as being eaten in Matabeleland. When I asked her why, she responded with gusto. *"AmaNdebele athanda inyama"* (The Ndebele people are great meat eaters).

Dancing commenced once we had finished our beefy supper. The drums, accompanying the Njelele type of songs, blared into the dark night sky. This was music for the indigenous people, those that the Ndebele people of Mzilikazi Khumalo found in this part of the world.

Later, the more martial Ndebele music took over. I had already retired to bed, in the car. However, my spiritual ear feasted on the Ndebele music that played virtually throughout the night. This was a night long bash. Dance, beef and beer carried the people to the next day. When I woke up the next morning, I was met by weary people who yearned for a quick nap in order to be ready for the second phase of the ceremony.

Here I came face to face with the spirit of Africa. The spirit of togetherness. That spirit of solidarity in bad and good times. Civilisation, that dehumanising condition of man, eats away at this very Africanness that has nurtured its people from time immemorial.

From about 10 o'clock in the morning there was a steady stream of neighbours bringing calabashes of beer. Scotch carts, pulled by four donkeys all walking side by side, brought in plastic containers of beer. I counted no less than 15 scotch carts that had come to deliver the beer to this homestead. Those coming on foot, both men and women, entered the homestead singing. At three o'clock in the afternoon, we took out of one hut a huge ilala basket into which was poured consecrated beer. This was the start of *izinyanga*. People moved and sang around the basket. My father was the first to step out of the circle and take a sip of beer using a gourd, *isiphungo*. What was left in the *isiphungo* he spilt to the ground and rejoined the singing and dancing group. More and more people followed suit until there was very little beer left in the basket.

Meanwhile, my father used a stick to stab the roof of the hut where the dance was taking place. He pulled out a little grass and threw it to the ground. This was an adulteration of an old Ndebele practice. In the past, the hut would have been completely destroyed.

The little beer remaining in the basket was poured on the ground. I inverted the basket and placed the gourd on it. More and more people poured into the homestead to take part in this great ceremony. Four beasts were slaughtered and eaten – the little girl from Josiah Chinamano School was right.

Mzilikazi in Zululand

Mzilikazi Khumalo was born in the 1790s in the Nquthu area of northern Nguni country in Eastern South Africa. This was before the emergence of multi-clan and powerful nation states. Society then was organised into small clans. The Khumalos, a Ntungwa Nguni group, lived under Magagu Wesikhaba Khumalo. There were other Khumalos in areas such as Enondweni, Empangeni, Emzinyathini and Ebabanango. For some unknown reason, the Khumalos under Magagu decided to leave the area north of Nquthu. Before this movement to the north, Mzilikazi and his twin brother, Bheje, were born. There is no agreement as to who their mother was. Patriarchal societies paid less attention to mothers.

Generally, South African sources, drawing mostly from the Reverend A T Bryant's *Olden Times in Zululand,* give the name of Mzilikazi's mother as Nomphethu, the daughter of Zwide KaLanga, the Ndwandwe (Nxumalo) king. Zimbabwean sources (Nyathi, 1994, Cobbing, 1976) claim that Mzilikazi's mother was Cikose Ndiweni, a daughter of the Mangwe chief, Ndlovu, who was the son of Mkheswa.

It is known that King Zwide Nxumalo killed Mzilikazi's father Matshobana. Was Zwide so callous that he could kill his son-in-law? Mzilikazi married Mwaka Nxumalo (Nkulumane's mother), who was King Zwide Nxumalo's daughter. If Mzilikazi's mother was a daughter of King Zwide Nxumalo, it would mean that Mzilikazi married his 'mother' by marrying Mwaka.

Nomphethu is likely to have been one of Mwaka's maids, alongside Fulatha Tshabalala. King Mzilikazi married Fulatha after 1826 following the death of Sukhunyana, Zwide's son and successor.

The case for Cikose being Mzilikazi's mother seems very strong. The Ndiwenis, being the King's maternal uncles, enjoyed a special place in the Ndebele State. When Mzilikazi Khumalo split his followers into two groups after their defeat by the Boers in 1837, one group was placed under the charge of Gundwane Ndiweni. King Mzilikazi Khumalo appointed several Ndiwenis as chiefs, for example Mpukane (for Usaba); Thambo (Inhlambabaloyi); Manyoba (Umhlanjwana); Mqengana (Emadibeni); Qaqa (Mhlahlandlela-kwesincane). Also, King Mzilikazi Khumalo is not known to have married another Ndiweni wife. Hilda Kuper cites a Northern Nguni custom that regards as preferential a marriage of a man to a woman of his own mother's patri-clan. Among the Ndebele, this preference seems to apply to a man's grandmother's patri-clan. That this was the practice is confirmed by Lobengula marrying Ndiwenis: Mpoliyana Ndiweni (Mabuyana's daughter and mother of Njube), Sitswapha Ndiweni (Mpini's sister and mother of Nguboyenja) and Mahwe Ndiweni (daughter of Mletshe, the chief of uJinga).

Usually, when a King's praises are rendered, there is reference to his mother's identity. For example, King Lobengula Khumalo's praises had this line – *Isilwane esimnyama sakoMabindela* (Nyathi, unpublished). Mabindela was the father of Fulatha Tshabalala, Lobengula's mother. King Mzilikazi Khumalo's praises, as given by Mdamba Khumalo, do make reference to his mother's people.

Inkosi yakithi yaphum'eMangweni kaMkheswa ka Ndlovu Ilayeni ngoba iyithulani MaZulu akeliyilondoloze (Nyathi, 1994).

At the time when the Khumalos settled in the Mkhuze area, far reaching political changes were taking place in South Africa. Powerful nation states were emerging. Matshobana and his relatives soon found themselves coming under the growing Ndwandwe State of Zwide Nxumalo. The state was to the east of the Khumalo area. To the south-east were the Mthethwa (Godongwana).

Zwide Nxumalo had Dingiswayo, chief of the Mthethwa, killed. But before the Mthethwa State was destroyed, Tshaka Zulu emerged and embraced it. Now King Zwide Nxumalo wanted to kill Tshaka Zulu through trickery. The Khumalo chiefs Donda and Matshobana informed Tshaka about Zwide's plans. Zwide, angered by the treachery of Donda Wesiziba and Matshobana, had the Khumalo chiefs killed. Matshobana had his arm removed. It is said King Zwide Nxumalo used it to concoct medicines with which he fortified himself (*ukutshwana*).

Following Matshobana's death in 1816, Mzilikazi returned to take over the chieftainship previously held by his father. Meanwhile, Zwide decided to attack Tshaka. The first fight, when Mzilikazi was on Zwide's side, took place in about 1818 at Qokli Hill. Before the next battle, Mzilikazi deserted Zwide and sought refuge under Tshaka. In 1819 King Zwide Nxumalo launched another attack on Tshaka who resorted to a scorched earth policy. His soldiers retreated, but made sure there was no food for Zwide Nxumalo's soldiers who were pursuing them. King Tshaka Zulu mounted a counter attack into Ndwandwe territory.

Mzilikazi was a capable leader who won Tshaka's admiration. He lived at Bulawayo, Tshaka's capital on the Mkhumbane River, for several years. He may have been placed in the frontline of Tshaka's soldiers, which included such people as Mncumbatha Khumalo and Mhlonga Thebe. The latter, a son of Nkolotsha, later became known as Mkhithika, 'feller of people', as a result of his military prowess.

King Tshaka began to grow fearful and jealous of the illustrious Mzilikazi who commanded some of the best men in the land. If Mzilikazi did turn against King Zwide Nxumalo, what would stop him from turning against King Tshaka? Consequently, King Tshaka planned to get rid of Mzilikazi. He sent him on a raid on the Sotho Chief Somnisi. Mzilikazi was deliberately given old soldiers in the hope that he and his aging army would be routed and killed. It was not to be. Mzilikazi and his army climbed a mountain and beat their shields, shouting *"impi kaTshaka isifikile!"* The intimidated Sotho ran helter skelter leaving behind their cattle that Mzilikazi quickly drove away.

The Sotho were well-known for possessing multi-coloured cattle called *amabhidi* in Ndebele. Such cattle were the envy of the Nguni. Enterprising Mzilikazi cut off the tail of one such beast, *eyamadlozi*, and doctored it with herbs. This, in his mind, would enable him to capture Sotho cattle. The black-eyed *amabhidi* cattle (*ezamehlo amnyama*) he captured became an aggravating factor in the animosity between Mzilikazi and King Tshaka Zulu, resulting in the former's flight from Zululand in about 1821.

Mzilikazi was circumcised at the time when he undertook the raid on the Sotho. The practice among the northern Nguni was to organise boys due for circumcision into age sets, *amabutho*. Later, especially under Tshaka, the age sets became militarised. It is thought that Lobengula Khumalo was among the last Ndebele men to be circumcised. By the 1880s circumcision was confined to the royal family. Prior to this, men did not marry until they were circumcised. This suggests that Mzilikazi left Zululand before he married. Between 1821 (when he left Zululand) and 1826 (when he married Mwaka) he married four wives. Some of his sons by these wives were Mangwana (by MaDlodlo), Muntu (by MaSigola), Qalingana (by Masuku) and Lopila (by MaFuyane). It is generally accepted that these sons did not qualify for succession because they were born before Mzilikazi became King. Only a King begets another King. This could confirm the suggestion that when Mzilikazi left Zululand he was not a King, but merely a leader of a wandering band. It was during this wandering that he was elevated, *ukwenyaswa*, to the status of King.

The treasures of Old Bulawayo

As we approach the summit of the low hill, we encounter a robust palisade made from mopane wood. The incomplete palisade sets the Royal Enclosure apart from the Peripheral Settlement, where the rest of the town dwellers lived. Several beehive huts have also been reconstructed.

Marieke Faber Clarke, Wilson Lethizulu Fuyana, Hudson Halimana Ndlovu and myself are visiting Old Bulawayo, or simply koBulawayo in the SiNdebele language. Marieke, who has been engaged in the research of Lozikeyi Dlodlo, is keen to see the latest developments on the Old Bulawayo project. She was last here in 1996.

Since her last visit a lot of groundwork has been covered. Archaeologists are busy at work. We have come to share ideas about their recent finds. A hut floor close to the presumed entrance has been exposed. Whose hut was it and what was it used for? Important finds of clay figurines have been unearthed by the excavators working at the site, which warrant careful ethnographic interpretation.

Old Bulawayo was established in 1870 as King Lobengula Khumalo's new capital. Mzilikazi Khumalo, the founding king of the Ndebele nation, died in 1868 and his remains were interred at Entumbane in the Matopo Hills. Mcumbatha Khumalo, son of Kholo, acted as regent until the contested accession to the throne by Lobengula. The Ndebele State was thrown into a bitter and bloody civil war in which some elements, led by Mbiko Masuku, umfokaMadlenya, the Chief of Zwangendaba, resisted Lobengula's assumption of the reins of power.

Lobengula Khumalo named his new capital town Gibixhengu, in memory of an earlier town built by Gundwane Ndiweni and his people when they settled in the Esigodini area in about 1839-40. In 1870, Lobengula, already a mature married man, came with his sister Mncengence to establish the new seat of power for the Ndebele.

Following the civil war of 1871-72, Lobengula, who emerged victorious, renamed his capital koBulawayo. *Obulawayo* is a singular form referring to the King himself. Where such a person, *obulawayo*, resides, is referred to as *kobulawayo*. Ko- is a locative formative. KoBulawayo, therefore, means the place where he (the King) who is being rejected (as evidenced by the civil war) resides.

This is the origin of the name koBulawayo, which had nothing to do with Tshaka's Bulawayo in Zululand. The similarity lay in the circumstances under which both men became kings - both faced initial rejection and opposition (*ukubulawa*) but went on to rule. Lobengula was born in about 1833 in the Marico Valley in the north-western Transvaal. And that was about 13 years after Mzilikazi Khumalo had left Zululand.

KoBulawayo does not mean a place of slaughter, as suggested in some colonial history books. The Jesuit missionaries who arrived in 1879 called it Gubulawayo. This was very close indeed if we take cognisance of the fact that, in those days, the 'K' sound was represented by the letter 'G'. Pronunciation was dictated by the context. Outside the old church building at Hope Fountain are the following words – UGUTULA KUBE KINI LONKE. Using the current Ndebele orthography UGUTULA would be written as UKUTHULA.

I would like to offer some tentative interpretation regarding the figurines that were unearthed by the archaeologists working at Old Bulawayo. Edward Matenga, a fundi on figurines, defines these cultural relics as 'Three dimensional miniature models of humans, animals and other objects' (Matenga, 1997). It would appear that among the Shona, figurines went beyond their intrinsic and aesthetic value. They assumed some significance in the Shona fertility ideology. Initial ethnographic findings do not reveal a similar situation among the Ndebele.

The clay figurines found at Old Bulawayo depict cattle and human beings. Among the Ndebele, moulding of figurines using clay was undertaken by children. It was part of *amandlwana* (child play). The games played by Ndebele children miniaturised adult activities.

Boys' *amandlwana* embraced moulding, with clay, of figurines such as those unearthed at Old Bulawayo. As a children's play activity, making figurines was carried out away from adults. It was undertaken either near or beyond the fence of the homestead. The boys, as future herdboys, moulded mostly cattle. There was differentiation among the cattle they made: oxen (with long horns, *impondo ezichayileyo*) and bulls (characterised by humps, shorter and sharper horns, *impondo ezithiyileyo*, and genitals, *isisende*).

Sometimes the cows were provided with calves – represented by smaller clay figurines without horns. Beasts so moulded were usually given names. Commonly, the names depicted colour or horn configuration. The cattle figurines, especially the bulls, were made to fight, *ukuqhutshezwa*. The owner or moulder bellowed on behalf of his clay bull – hence the saying *ukukhonyelwa njengenkomo yomdaka* (his master's voice).

In real life, the more grown up herdboys enjoyed and encouraged bull fights.

The boys whistled wildly, *ukutshotsholozela.* The bulls responded by bellowing all the louder. Then the excited boys recited the praises of their bulls, *ukutema inkunzi.* The following lines serve as an example of a bull's praises.

Ubobukel'
UmfokaBhembe
Umfoka ndum' ezimabala
Uchopho bekiti
Iphaphu lentwala

The age-set leaders, *ingqwele,* taught the younger boys various games, including praises such as those given above.

Sometimes acacia tree thorns were pushed into the head to serve as horns. It was also common to find boys using tubers, through which a forked piece of wood was pushed, as bulls, called *inkunzi zamagudu. Igudu* is the tuber used in conjunction with the forked wood during the making of bull figurines. Figurines made from such materials do not last long, either above or below ground level.

Clay figurines were either fired, *ukutshiswa,* or not fired. Generally, children were not allowed to fire their figurines - for fear of them starting veld fires. However, when their mothers or grandmothers fired their clay pots, using dry cow dung, the children could add their figurines.

During the period before colonisation, beads were a prized possession. Adults, especially women, used them as adornments. Some beads were small, *ubuhlalu,* while others were big, *amangqongqo.* Children used scrap items during their various games. Small beads could have been used to represent eyes during the moulding of clay figurines.

The presence of such beads should not suggest any ritual significance. Where Christianity took a strong foothold after colonisation, beads came to be associated with paganism. Their use as objects of adornment was abandoned. They ceased to be objects that people sought.

In addition to cattle figurines, the boys made human figurines. To indicate sex, female figurines were provided with little bulges on the chest. The male figurines were sometimes made to ride on the cattle figurines. Riding, *ukugada inzomba,* was common among the boys.

Elaborate Ndebele marriage rites

Ukucola was an important concept among the Ndebele. The word *cola* means to cleanse (*hlambulula, geza, hlambulula inhliziyo*), to express happiness (*ukuthokoza okupheleleyo)* and to wish one success.

Subsumed in the concept is to acknowledge, accept and bless. There are several instances in the lives of the Ndebele when *ukucola* was performed. A newborn baby, who was believed to belong to the ancestors, went through the ritual.

A new king, on being crowned, went through *ukucolwa* ritual. The new king had to be announced to the ancestral community, who were expected to shower the new monarch with blessings.

Ukucola was an important ritual in Ndebele marriage rites. Marriage among the Ndebele was a complex, protracted series of rites involving a wide spectrum of people - the living and the living dead.

A day before the marriage party departed for the groom's home, the bride-to-be's father slaughtered a goat, ox or cow with which to *cola* his daughter. The father personally anointed her with the bile from the slaughtered animal, *inyongo*. There are special parts of the body where *inyongo* was applied, the top part of the head, *enkanda,* back of the neck, *izonga*, limb joints, *amalunga*, such as elbows, knees, ankles and wrists and toes. The process was known as *ukuthela inyongo* and it had spiritual implications. The bitter, yellowish green substance worked as some kind of libation to the departed ancestors, *abaphansi.*

The father, as the religious focus of both the material (living) and spiritual (departed ancestors) families, informed all parties of the marriage contract. He, on their behalf, acceded to and blessed the arrangement. On the young woman's side, marriage meant subtraction or loss of an individual. Departed ancestors, who had an interest in the welfare of their progeny, had to be informed. When a bride left her father's home on getting married, her father informed the living dead that a subtraction was being made to their family

There were both physical and spiritual dimensions to the process of tying the knot. The ancestors would continue to look after their own blood. *Ukucola* thus became a prayer and an appeal to them not to relinquish their responsibilities.

The day following the initial rites, the wedding party, *umthimba,* left for the groom's home. The bride and her father entered the cattle byre where the latter performed another rite known as *ukuphehlela isthundu.* The father used a stirring device, *uphehlo*, to vigorously stir the contents of a gourd until a white foam was produced. The white froth was poured over his daughter's head, neck, and body. Simultaneously, he appealed to the departed ancestors to look after his daughter.

The girl left the cattle byre, not through the entrance, *isango*, but through the fence, *umbelo*. She was handed a knife by her father or brother.

Prior to the marriage taking place, the girl would have visited her relatives to inform them and bid them farewell. Some would have given her gifts and beasts to be slaughtered during her *umcolo*. The animals could have been goats or cattle, depending on the relatives' wealth.

The empty gall bladder from the father's beast was blown up, using *umsingazana* or *usezi* grasses, and tied with a string. It was then hung around the neck of a bridesmaid, *usonyongwana* (Interview with Hudson Halimana Ndlovu, 2000).

Meanwhile, the wedding party sang, *ukuklaza,* as it received and followed the bride-to-be, who bowed her head and became, from that point on, a bride, *umlobokazi.*

As she walked away her team of close associates moved closely around her – almost concealing her. These associates included the matron*, igqwele*, the bridesmaids, *usonyongwana*, and those who swept the groom's village, *osomthanyelwana.*

Subtraction or separation on the bride's side had to be counterbalanced by addition or incorporation on the groom's side. In practical terms, the groom's people had to *cola* the bride to achieve her incorporation. The groom's departed ancestors were involved in the process.

On arrival, the wedding party completely surrounded the bride to block her from public view, *umthimba usungumtshitshi*. It was feared that her footsteps would be stolen, *ukucutshwa inyawo*, and magically worked upon to harm her. Reed mats were placed along the path, *ukudaya amancansi*. This could have been an honour, but also forestalled attempts to steal her footprints.

After protracted exchanges at the cattle byre, *isibaya,* the wedding party entered the groom's village. The party remained standing until a beast was paid to facilitate their sitting down, *inkomo yamacansi.*

The bride remained behind as her party went into the groom's cattle byre to be shown the beast that was to be slaughtered to *cola* the bride. A man from the groom's side was chosen to stab the beast.

Meanwhile, the bride crossed her feet, *ukwelekanisa inyawo*, in an effort to prevent the stabbed beast from falling to the ground. Should the man from the groom's side fail to fell the beast, the spear was then handed over to a man from the bride's side. After the stabbing, the spear was cleaned thoroughly using cattle manure, *umquba*. The bladder from the beast was blown up and worn around the neck by *usonyongwana*.

The bride dressed up for the *ukumekeza* ceremony. She wore a crown, *amantiya,* which consisted of beautiful feathers like those of *ifefe* or *ijuba.* She applied some powder, *isibhuda,* to her face and decorative designs were made, *ukubalaza* or *ukuloba.*

The height of the wedding ceremony consisted of *ukumekeza,* the bridal dance that took place in the cattle byre. The bride's assistants, *osomthanyelwana,* danced first. Then the bride came, holding in one hand the knife given by her father and in the other hand *indabula*, made from well-trimmed grass. It resembled a broom (Interview with Hudson Halimana Ndlovu). The bride advanced towards the groom and requested him to join in the dance. As she danced, her head and neck moved back and forth, *ukukhupha umqalo.*

The two danced together for a while until the matron, *ingqwele*, using a short stick, tapped the bride on the back. The act signalled the end of *ukumekeza.*

When all was over, the party departed on its way back home. One thing the party did on its return was to remove *imincwazi,* bands of skin or cloth worn around the head, *ukwethula imicwazi* (Nyathi, 2001).

Usonyongwana remained behind to assist the bride. After three weeks, the bride and her *usonyangwana* returned home, *ukuphinda imikhondo.* The purpose was three fold. The bride's people shaved off her hair and left a top knot, *ukukhehla icholo* or *ukubekwa icholo. Icholo* was worn by married women.

Secondly, the return afforded her the chance to pick up the gifts given to her by her relatives. The gifts would have been given her when she undertook a visit to bid them farewell.

Finally, the occasion was used to burn the gall bladders that *usonyongwana* were wearing. This involved bladders from both the bride's and groom's sides. The bladders were placed in a potsherd, *udengezi,* and burnt together in a way that symbolised the creation of a lasting relationship between the groom's and the bride's families - both material (living) and spiritual (of departed ancestors).

This was the final spiritual and physical tying of the knot – the Ndebele way. The ashes of the burnt bladders were deposited on the midden, *esilotheni. Ifindo lenja Batayi!*

Sometimes, in exceptional circumstances, a wedding party failed to return home to have the bands removed. This was the case when Mwaka, Nkulumane's mother, married King Mzilikazi Khumalo. They remained since there was a good life to be lived at the royal residence, with plenty of food. The village the party lived in became known as Umncwazi, in reference to not having had the bands removed. Here Mtotobi Mlilo, son of Nkumba, became chief. Umncwazi was the village where one of King Mzilikazi Khumalo's queens known as Nyembezana Thebe lived. Her son, Ndanisa, later known as Nyanda, was born in that village which, in 1847, had been attacked by Boer forces under the command of Andries Hendrick Potgieter.

Polygamy for a special purpose

When the *Sunday News* published an article about Mr Italy Khumalo, who wed two brides, many people took a keen interest. While some hailed Khumalo for reviving an old Ndebele custom, others were not amused. The marriage arrangement in question was no ordinary polygamy, which is still alive in Zimbabwe today. Rather, it was about how that polygamy came about.

Before delving into the matter, it is appropriate to note certain relevant principles pertaining to marriage. Marriage was a contract, not between two spouses, but between two families. The families extended to include the departed ancestors. In this regard, it was not only the husband who had an interest in the bride, the extended family also did.

Marriage was an economic contract between the two families. The bride's family received lobola, usually in the form of cattle, in exchange for their daughter, who was viewed as a provider of labour through the children she would bear for the groom's family. This arrangement is what one author has called 'cattle for wives'.

As implied above, the most important function of the marriage institution was to bring children into the world – hence the bride was told '*ufike uveze abantu*' or '*ufike ugenquke*'. The wife's worth was determined by, among other considerations, whether or not she bore children for the groom's family.

The bride's family benefited from the marriage of their daughter. The bride's father, under normal circumstances, would give a beast to each of his brothers. This is called *ukutshayela abafowenu*.

The inability to produce children, by either husband or wife, was socially resolved. Not having children carried a stigma that was avoided at all cost. Arrangements were made to circumvent the problem.

The bride's family had an obligation to ensure that their daughter bore children for her husband's family. Should their daughter prove to be barren, another of their daughters, almost always younger, would take over the function of bearing children for her. The process is called *ukuvusa amaseko*. The critical belief was that '*imuzi ngumuzi ngomlilo*'. Children are the expected result of a marriage.

Related to this was the fact that marriage was an irreversible contract. Only witchcraft and adultery, and probably insanity, were enough reason to nullify the contract. The bride's people, having taken delivery of the wealth of lobola, did not want to lose it. Hence the saying '*lizidle lizibeke amathambo*' ('eat them, but keep the bones'). To avoid the husband demanding back the cattle, his in-laws sent him a compensatory wife.

Such a wife was called *inhlanzi*. She could be a younger sister of the barren wife, her brother's daughter, her maternal uncle's daughter (*umzawakhe*) or her paternal uncle's daughter. When the father-in-law had no other daughters to be given away as *inhlanzi*, his brothers, by accepting *ukutshayelwa*, obligated themselves to providing a substitute.

Two different cases of how *inhlanzi* came about need elaboration. The first case was when, during the marriage, the bride was given a maid specifically to take care of the eventuality of barrenness. This occurred especially when the daughter was being married into a rich family and there was a lot at stake by way of wealth.

A good example is when Mwaka Nxumalo, Nkulumane's mother, got married to King Mzilikazi. The Nxumalos sent, among other maids, Fulatha Tshabalala, who was Mwaka's cousin. If Mwaka had proved barren, Fulatha would have borne the heir to the throne. Mzilikazi and Fulatha did have a child, Lobengula, and the latter's claim to the Ndebele throne was based on this marriage custom, with Nkulumane having disappeared.

In the more common form, *inhlanzi* was sent (notice the initiative was taken by the barren wife's family) after barrenness had been proved. If after two or three years the wife had not conceived, *engaphathanga*, it was concluded she was barren. In Ndebele they would say *inyoka yakhe kayithathi* and various herbal formulations would be tried. The husband would also be given, in an earthen pot, *imbiza* in order to 'sharpen' him, *ukumlola* or *ukumcandula*.

The wife sometimes went back to her own family and on arrival, wailed and rolled herself on the ground, *bangenze isiduli*. They have turned me into an anthill. *Ngiswele lesikhusukhuswana.* I can't get a child. *Bangicuyile.* They have bewitched me. Her family would discuss which girl to give as her *inhlanzi*.

It was left to the husband whether or not to pay lobola, even if only a little. *Inhlanzi* was coming to compensate for her relative's infertility. Important to note here is the fact that the woman took the initiative to find her own relative to bear children for her. The eldest boy would normally be brought up by the senior wife and inherit his late father's estate and position as if he (the son) was born by the senior (but barren) wife.

A few well known examples may be cited. Queen Lozikeyi Dlodlo, the daughter of Ngogo of Enqameni, and King Lobengula's wife, had no issue.

Her paternal uncle, Mletshe Dlodlo, gave her *inhlanzi* called Mamfimfi. The daughter born by this *inhlanzi,* and technically regarded as Lozikeyi's daughter, was Sidambe, who later married Siyatsha Fuyane. Their daughter was Pombo.

Another example is that of Mbhida Mkhwananzi who was married by King Lobengula. When Mbhida could not conceive, the Mkhwananzis gave Mbhida an *inhlanzi* called Mfaziwamajaha. No sooner had Mfaziwamajaha been married to King Lobengula than Mbhida fell pregnant with Nyamande. Mfaziwamajaha's child was called Mhlambi, whose fate is shrouded in mystery, just like Nkulumane's.

Icholo and other wifely adornments

"You, son of Menyezwa, how can I have *icholo* (the top knot)? You know its owner is late," says the 79-year old Mrs. Thina Maphosa (nee Ncube), whose husband died a few years ago. Mrs. Maphosa, also known as Naka Onah, was born in the Gwandavale area whose headman was Maxolo Mathema of Enqameni. The chief of Enqameni at the time was Ndanisa Khumalo. MaNcube has spent most of her active life at Sankonjana, but in 1998 she relocated to the Gula or Tshapho area in the Matopo Hills. I have visited her to gather some information on a dying Ndebele cultural practice – leaving a tuft of hair, *icholo,* at the back of a married woman's head.

"When we were young girls, as soon as a woman had a child, she wore *icholo,*" says MaNcube. "However, *icholo* was mostly worn by a married woman, *inina,*" adds MaNcube, whose strength belies her age.

Hudson Halimana, a guru on Ndebele traditional practices, has this to say. "When a young woman got married, she wore an over-shoulder band, *umgaxo.* This was a sign of respect for her in-laws. In addition, the bride also wore some solid fat, *ihwahwa,* at the back of her head, which was liberally festooned with multicoloured beads and feathers."

In fact, the fat was placed exactly where *icholo* would be located. After the marriage dance, *ukumekeza,* in the company of her maid, *usonyongwana,* she went back to her people. It was during the visit that *icholo* was fashioned. At the instigation of her father, a razor, *insingo,* removed all the hair, *ukuqwatha,* save for a tuft at the back of her head. In days gone by, a white stone was split and its sharp edges were used to scrape off the hair. Water was used during the process. Later, with the introduction of glass bottles, a broken piece of glass was used to achieve the same result. An aunt, mother or elder sister shaved the hair and this was done outside the homestead. Hair so cut was deposited into a hole in the ground, *umhome.*

The top knot, *icholo,* was said to belong to the husband. It was a mark to indicate the marital status of the woman. *Icholo* was the equivalent of the modern wedding ring. Other men were not allowed to proposition her or joke with her in a suggestive manner.

When the young wife went back to her new husband's home, her father-in-law suggested, through his wife, that the young woman should remove the over-shoulder band. *Icholo* sufficed as a sign of respect.

The young woman who had attained a new status was referred to as, for example, MaKhumalo, MaNcube, MaNyathi. When she had a child she was referred to as Naka Sibhijo, Naka Sigqumfemfe etc. It was also common, in the early days, to call a married woman by her father's name, for example, okaSwalubuyo (Swalubuyo's daughter).

When *icholo* grew long it was trimmed, but never removed completely. Only when the husband died, *isihlahla sesiwile*, would it be removed. The rest of the hair was not shaved. The widow wore a band around her head, *isincwazi*. This band warned would–be suitors to keep off – she was in mourning.

A year later, during *umbuyiso*, the bringing home of the spirit ceremony, two things happened. If the widow had no intention of remarrying, her hair was shaved and a new *icholo* was created. This *icholo* was more of an expression of a senior status and respect for the children, *umthunzi wabantwana*, rather than an indicator of 'protected territory'. However, to express her intention not to get married again, she wore *isincwazi* tied high around the head. Its position differed from that of the band to express the condition of bereavement. This one did not pass over the face.

Many of King Lobengula's widows, who opted not to be remarried, wore *izincwazi*. Some of the widows were Lozikeyi, Mpoliyana, Somadiko and Dingowabo (Nyathi, 1999). However, some widows opted to remarry. Sitshwapha Ndiweni got married to Mtshane Khumalo, Fakubi to Manyoba Ndiweni and Mfubezi to Malevu Magutshwa.

If the widow chose to marry her late husband's younger brother, *ukungenwa*, she did not wear *isincwazi*. A new *icholo* was created and it now belonged to her new husband.

After a divorce, the woman could have *icholo* removed - by her husband's people. However if, for some reason, they could not do it, they gave permission to the divorcee's parents to do so. The bottom line is that authority had to be given by her in-laws. The divorced woman took her children along with her, if lobola had not been paid. If lobola had been paid, she left the children behind; they contractually belonged to the husband.

Changes have caught up with this age-old Ndebele custom, which has, generally, been abandoned. A headcover, *iqhiye*, has replaced *icholo* as a symbol of respect, particularly during funerals or in the presence of a woman's in-laws. For example, Mrs. Thina Maphosa had her *icholo* removed. She had come to perceive it as *uphondo*, an unwelcome protuberance from her head. Her husband, Fever Maphosa, as the owner of *icholo*, shaved it. Before I bid her farewell, she reminds me that my two mothers still have their *amacholo*. "Why didn't you ask them?" She quizzes me. Silence.

Pregnancy and marriage

Normally, a young woman got married before falling pregnant. As a general rule, safe sex was practised – *ukuhlobonga*, or *ukuphelela emathangazini*. When an unmarried woman became pregnant, she, in the company of her aunt, went to announce her pregnancy to the parents of the father of the baby, *ukubikwa kwesisu*. If there was no aunt available, an elder sister could be a substitute. The women sat outside the young man's village until their presence was noticed. A relative was chosen to approach them and inquire as to their business. Both the aunt and her niece did not smile, *bayasinama*. In fact, there were no greetings exchanged between them and the emissary. The women simply said, "*Sizebika umthwalo*" (We have come to announce the load). The emissary then quizzed them as to who was the culprit and they responded with the offender's name.

The young man's father then summoned his son to quiz him on the allegation levelled against him. "Do you know what business brings them here?"

If the young man accepted responsibility, *umthwalo ngowami*, the two women were ushered into the village where they were accommodated for the night. It was only at this juncture that the two parties exchanged greetings and smiles. In the morning, the young man's father would bring them a live goat. The father then took responsibility. His son's sins were his. *Inyoni itshayelwa abadala*. The young man's crime belonged to the father and hence to the village.

"*Nansi isifuyo esicola ngaso umthwalo wethu.*" (Here is the beast with which I acknowledge and accept responsibility for the pregnancy.) (Interview with Hudson Halimana Ndlovu, 2000)

The aunt thanked the father for the beast, which was then slaughtered and its meat consumed. Its skin was spread out and fixed to the ground by sharpened wooden pegs, *izikhonkwane*. The women stayed at the village for one more night to allow the hide to dry. The following day the hide, *isikhumba*, was folded and tied by a string.

"*Nansi mntwana azangcaya ngaso umthwalo wethu,*" said the father as he presented the folded skin for carrying the baby to the aunt. The skin would be tanned, *ukutshukwa*, and used as a maternity dress, *ingcayo*. The aunt and her niece then went back home.

When the woman had given birth, word was sent to the young man's parents. They in turn dispatched someone, usually the young man's mother, to congratulate the new mother, *ikwenza amhlophe*. The young man's parents may then have sent another beast to be slaughtered. The young woman's father may also have slaughtered a goat for his daughter.

The beast provided meat for the baby, *inyama yomntwana*. In reality, it was meat for the mother who, it was believed, after eating the meat, would produce more milk. Sometimes the goat was referred to as *imbuzi yokukhupha itshatha* (a goat for removing the stain).

A pregnancy before marriage could have had implications for inheritance. If the young man accepted the pregnancy, his son, if the eldest, could inherit his father's wealth and position in the family. He became *indlalifa*. The young woman may then still perform the *ukumekeza* dance as she was regarded as being a full *intombi*. This contrasts with an *imitha*, one who has already had a baby, who was not allowed to *mekeza*.

However, if the young man decided not to marry her, she became *imitha* and her son did not become *indlalifa*. The young woman could not perform *ukumekeza*. The young man's father could decide to pay something to take custody of his grandson – who would have been living with his mother. This was called *ukuhlenga*. *Ukuhlenga* differed from payment of lobola in that the former was paid when the mother was not married.

A young woman who already had a child could get married, albeit with reduced status, *ulolufa*. Her father could remove the stigma, *ukwesula ubutshapha*, by payment of a beast to restore his daughter to the status of a full *intombi*. This was known as *ukugcwalisa*. If the young man's parents accepted the beast, the first born son became *indlalifa*. On getting married, the young woman was usually accompanied by one person. She did not perform the *ukumekeza* dance. It was a low-key wedding.

There were instances when woman brought another man's child into a marriage. The husband could have decided to conceal the child's identity in order not to embarrass both the child and her mother. In this case, the son or daughter could use the husband's surname, but the spirits would not know the illegitimate son and would not accept him. It is the *indlalifa* who should hold the spear at his father's internment and thus become the bridge, the all important spiritual link between the living and the living dead.

All about 'Matshayisikhova' - from a mobile library

Wrinkles on both his face and neck bear testimony to his advanced age. Grey hair and feeble footsteps complete the picture of one who has witnessed many Christmases. He is Nyumbana Dube of Sankonjana in Sear Block, Matobo District. He and his family came to Sankonjana in 1943.

"I came here at the same time as your father who was coming from Nkonyane," says Dube. "Here we found Mhlatshwa Ncube, Nzibane Ncube, Silebuho Nyathi and Sitshela Nyathi. The first two are Kalanga who came from across the Shashani River. The last two are Birwa by origin. They also came from across the Shashani River. There were also men like Manja Nyathi, Motsamayi Nyathi, Zintsere Mdlongwa, Thatha Ngulube and Phulu Mguni. These came before us. They are the pioneers of Sankonjana."

Sear Block fell under Chief Marahwane Ndiweni, the son of Sinti Ndiweni. Both he and his father were acting for the young Dumezweni, the son of Siqalaba Ndiweni and the grandson of Nyangazonke.

Though both Gijimani and Sinti were sons of Faku Ndiweni and MaThebe kaMkhithika, they could not succeed their father. Faku had later married Princess Nedlana, who bore him a son, Nyangazonke. By virtue of being the king's nephew, Nyangazonke took precedence over the older Gijimani and Sinti. Faku then built MaThebe her own home, as a result of which she was aptly named Khutshwekhaya ('Removed from home').

Silebuho Nyathi, who was a clever dip attendant, was appointed headman by the administration ahead of his elder brother Sitshela. Both men were descendants of the Birwa Chief Kgwatalala whose death was ordered by King Lobengula Khumalo in the 1870s over the Nkulumane affair. "Have you heard of *Umswiliswili wenkosi?*" inquires Mr Dube. I confirm that I have heard about him. Both the late Fiti Nare and my own father used to tell me about him. *Umswiliswi* is a bird that warns animals about impending danger. Hunters don't like it as it scares away the animals they are hunting.

Chief Kgwatalala had been appointed to become the eyes and ears of King Mzilikazi Khumalo. The King was afraid the Boers would attack him from the south. Indeed, Andries Hendrick Potgieter, uNdaleka, did invade Matabeleland in 1847.

Following the installation of Lobengula Khumalo in 1870, reports came that Nkulumane, the rightful heir, had arrived and was camped at Sizeze – an area under Chief Kgwatalala. Chief Kgwatalala reported this arrival to Chief Thunzi Ndiweni of Ezinaleni, and not directly to the King. Chief

Kgwatalala's report on Nkulumane failed to reach the King in Bulawayo. Consequently, Chief Kgwatalala and other Birwa chiefs were executed for seemingly failing in their role as *imiswiliswili yenkosi*.

Chief Thunzi Ndiweni was also executed in 1875 for supporting Nkulumane. Following his death, Faku Ndiweni became regent for Thunzi's son, Tala, who was the rightful heir. However, Faku entrenched himself in his position. King Lobengula Khumalo married Faku's sister Mpoliyana, Njube's mother. By later marrying Princess Nedlana and supporting the whites during Imfazo II, Faku secured the Ndiweni chieftainship.

The present chief, a son of Tapi, is Faku's great grandson. "Locanda Ndiweni tried to revive the issue of chieftainship after Dumezweni's death, but was decampaigned by Ntinima Ndiweni," claims Mr Nyumbana Dube, who has lived under three Ndiweni chiefs. Locanda Ndiweni was a direct descendant of the original Zisongo/Zinala Chief Thunzi – whose father was Mabuyana, the son of the famous Gundwane Ndiweni.

My interviewee, Nyumbana Dube, born on December 25 1907, grew up in the Fort Usher area, Efodini. His father, Tikitiki, left the Gulati area where Thekwane, Nyumbana's grandfather lived. They trace their origins to Hanana in Limpopo Province on the western fringes of the Soutpansberg mountains. Ntoba, the son of Nkwalabwani, was brought to this country by Goboyi Khumalo, the father of Nyovane – most probably as his captive.

"Let me tell you how I got my name. My father Tikitiki married MaLuphahla, who failed to conceive. Then my father married MaNdlovu, who bore me and my brother Major. One of his neighbours, Nyumbana Tshongwe, said to the people, 'You said Tikitiki was incapable of fathering a child. Now look, he has got a son. I shall name the son after myself'."

While a young boy, Nyumbana Dube faced eviction from the Fort Usher area. A white man took over their land and built himself a house, which today is part of Gulati School. Nyumbana Dube and his people were pushed to Gwandavale – also under Inqama chief, Ndanisa Khumalo, who initially belonged to the Hlalini village. The most famous and founding chief of Inqama was Somhlolo Mathema, who was succeeded by Dliso.

In 1927, Nyumbana Dube took driving lessons and qualified as a lorry driver. He subsequently got employment at New Mine where he served as a driver for the Chinese owners of the mine which was, accordingly, named Sun Yet Sen. At Sun Yet Sen, Nyumbana worked with a man from Lubhangwe, who alerted him to a pleasant sparsely populated place at Sankonjana. As a result of his job, Nyumbana Dube has come to be known as Driver or by the now more popular version of Mtirayi.

He still remembers a number of native commissioners at Fort Usher. "We called native commissioner Jackson, Matshayisikhova. Native commissioner Elliot was called uMabhedla. Then, there was uMahwanqa who was succeeded by Stewart. Another one that I still remember was Benzies (W.R.)."

Several people in the Gwanda and Matobo Districts got their names from the native commissioners. A lot more got their names from early missionaries, especially of the Brethren in Christ Church. No wonder there are names like Stikoti, Emma and Abbie.

"Do you want me to tell you the story about native commissioner uMatshayisikhova?' asks Mr Dube as he sips from a cup of tea. I nod and listen attentively.

"UMatshayisikhova arrived in Bulawayo and was fluent in Ndebele. He was deployed to the Fort Mlugulu office. Inqama chief admired his fluency in Ndebele and wanted to have him as native commissioner at Fort Usher.

"A team of men and woman and three oxen were dispatched to pick him up at Fort Mlugulu. Ntola Khumalo was then chief of uMzinyathi. Four men carried uMatshayisikhova on his bed. They made several stopovers along the way. Wherever they rested an ox was killed. The journey to Fort Usher lasted three days.

"On arrival at Fort Usher, uMatshayisikhova enquired from Inqama chief, 'Chief, I hear there is God here at Matojeni'.

'Indeed Nkosi, there is one and Dabha looks after the shrine,' responded the chief.

'I want to see him.'

'Well, there is his son Tategulu. He will take you to his father'.

"So, off the two went in a scotchcart so that uMatshayisikhova could see the much talked about God of Matojeni.

'Father, here is uNkosi, the native commissioner. He says he wants to see uMlimu (God)'. Turning now to uMatshayisikhova, Dabha said, 'Nkosi, you say you have come to see uMlimu?'

'Yebo Dabha,' replied the native commissioner. 'If he is not there, I warn you Dabha, you will go to prison.'"

Our animated conversation is at this juncture interrupted by my father, Menyezwa, who is busy preparing a dish of cooked blood, *ubende* (*ububende*). "Oh he (Nyumbana Dube) was a good driver. Even when the axle of my lorry came off, he was able to control the vehicle."

Nyumbana Dube continues with his story. "All of a sudden, there emerged two vicious dogs called Matshani. They lunched on the native commissioner's trousers, tearing them to shreds in the process.

'*Futseki* Matshani!' shouted Dabha.

"Dabha asked the terrified native commissioner, 'Nkosi, do you still wish to see uMlimu?' Undeterred, uMatshayisikhova responded in the affirmative.

'Come on then, let's go,' said Dabha.

'Remove your shoes, Nkosi,' demanded Dabha. 'Now, sit down, cross legged and repeat after me. Mbedzi! Thobela! And don't ever dare to look up.'

"Curious to see uMlimu, the native commissioner said to Dabha, 'Please Dabha, introduce me.'

'But how do I do it? You said you wanted to see uMlimu.'"

Nyumbana Dube smiles in disbelief. "Then uMatshayisikhova spoke to God in English. The two engaged in a long conversation in English. 'Nkosi, now pay. The red paper. Place it on the ground.' For a while the two were locked in a light-hearted conversation.

"Turning to the native commissioner Dabha said, 'Nkosi, look for your note'.

'My good Lord, I can't find it Dabha'.

"Then the voice came for the last time, 'Thank you Mr Jackson'."

Nyumbana Dube stands up and shakes my hand in farewell "Bye bye babazala!" he says.

"There goes a mobile library. Will I ever be so privileged again as to borrow a few books from it?" I ask myself. Only time will tell.

"Good bye *mkhwenyana*. Good bye Nkwite, so long Hana."

Evictees' cries of desperation fell on deaf ears

Throughout the night, government trucks droned and coughed. Their load of crying babies, bleating sheep, blaring goats and rattling pots produced a noise of misery, desperation and utter dejection. The noise, as expected, fell on deaf ears.

The anger of 46 years ago shows on the faces of my informants, who had been brutalised and traumatised by the experience.

"Were you lumped onto the lorries together with your cattle?" I ask. One man shakes his head frantically and, finally, supports it on his cupped hand. That's another sad story weighing heavily on the man.

Young men were asked to drive the cattle to Bulawayo, over 100 kilometres away. After four days weary march, they arrived in Bulawayo, where the cattle were loaded onto a train going to Victoria Falls.

One man grins, recalling the melodrama when the train pulled out on its way to Victoria Falls. One truck, which was supposed to carry the herdsmen, was not connected to the train. So off went the cattle, leaving behind the stranded and worried young men. Frantic efforts were made to reunite them with the cattle. Fortunately, a lorry was found to take them to Gwayi Siding, where they found the cattle penned in waiting for them. Meanwhile, the Government trucks had arrived in Lupane that morning. All the evictees (*amadelika*) were dumped at Mpahlwa Number One. They were expected to venture out into the surrounding bush to commence construction of new homes. This they would do once they had been reunited with their cattle.

Fatigued, grubby and hungry, the herdsmen drove their cattle from Gwayi Siding towards Mpahlwa Number One, a distance of over 60 kilometres. At this point the man whose head had all along been supported by his cupped palm gets up and curses, "*Mntanami, amakhiwa ...*"(My son, the white men ...).

In Lupane District there is a green plant that is highly noxious. They call it *umkhawuzane*. It is not found in the Matopo District. In September and October, the killer plant has green leaves that are irresistible to unschooled cattle from Maphaneni. On seeing this plant, the cattle went for it in a big way. The drivers, equally ignorant of its hazard, thought their cattle had stumbled upon good succulent foliage. The cattle died in their hundreds.

The goats and sheep at Mpahlwa Number One also fell for the deceptive plant. This was a devastating blow to the evictees. For them, their livestock was their lifeblood. This was a double tragedy that haunts them to this day.

Two men join us. One is Nyasa Nyathi, and the second is Marogwe, alias Masiketi. The second man's names mean the same thing. He gave the names to his donkeys, and now their names have become his. Nyasa Nyathi is quite a sight, a black sight I should say. He wears a black suit, black socks, black tie and a black shirt. His hair is pitch black. His story of eviction is an exception in that he did not come from Maphaneni in the Matopo District.

I enquire more about the conditions prevailing here in 1951. On arrival in the Lupane District, the evictees found that fields had already been surveyed and pegged out. Thatch grass had been collected. Boreholes had been sunk and a few more were sunk after their arrival.

There were no clinics when they arrived here. Later a clinic was built by the Catholics at St. Paul's Mission, on the Shangani River, which was an extension of St. Luke's.

There is a similar story with regard to schools. The colonial government just did not bother to put up schools for 'natives'. They left this function to the various church organisations. One year after their arrival, the Catholics built Mpahlwa Two and Three, and Pupu. Gobhi, the school nearest to where we are, was built by the Anglicans.

As far back as 1918, the Dipping Ordinance was already in place. In a letter to the Editor of the *Bulawayo Chronicle* of October 18, 1918, one farmer complained: "Now that our Dipping Ordinance is in force, who have Chartered Company made responsible for the dips in the natives reserves? For instance, I am farming near Indaba Duna native reserve and dip my cattle regularly every Saturday, yet the natives in this reserve have not dipped their cattle for seven weeks, owing to either the windmill having broken down or water troubles."

For these evictees dip tanks had been constructed at Gomoza and at Ndwana, across the Shangani River.

In terms of local administration, these people were placed under Chief Mabhika Khumalo, the son of Mlonyeni, kaThulwana, kaNtini, kaVala, kaMangethe, kaLunga. Nicholas Edwin Khumalo is the reigning Chief Mabhikwa. Their headman is Ngubo Moyo, who lives across the Shangani River.

Gogo Matshazi's slit ears 'mark' her as an Ndebele

Emma Mlotswa, better known as Gogo Matshazi, a grand-daughter of the famous Mfagilele Matshazi of the Indanana village, comes to meet me at her house in Luveve from her maize field at 'The Gumtrees'. What used to be maize fields nearby have become the suburb of Cowdray Park. Though weary after a long walk from the field, Gogo Matshazi is still able to greet me with a smile. We go through the usual ritual of exchanging warm greetings and quickly get down to business.

My eyes settle on her ears with their distinctive slits called *imikleklo*. This is a vanishing Ndebele cultural practice that I wish to know more about.

"You tell me your ears were not slit? Was your father too lazy to have your ears cut?" I quickly try to think of a face-saving response. I can't admit my father was lazy.

Gogo Matshazi was born in 1922 in the Gwatemba area of Filabusi. That was long before the establishment of Native Purchase Areas, since named small scale farming areas.

With the object of my visit explained, the ever obliging Gogo Matshazi takes me decades back to the time when she had her ears slit. She and her contemporaries from the locality, both male and female, were identified as candidates for the sharp knife. Ear slitting was an occasion to look forward to. It was one step in a series that led to full membership of Ndebele society.

Gogo Matshazi and her peers gathered very early in the morning on a winter's day. The time of day and season of year were carefully chosen. Low temperatures inhibit bacterial growth – thus reducing the chances of the fresh slits becoming festering wounds – and, perhaps, the victims of the knife endured less pain

The little children, displaying a mixture of apprehension and elation, were led to a homestead, where a man awaited them, armed with a sharp knife and short pieces of sorghum stalks – the topmost internodes called *ingaba*.

The man approached each child and placed a wooden support behind an ear. As the knife cut through the ear lobe, the little ones were warned against flinching. Stoicism was a celebrated trait among the Ndebele. Stoicism was certainly needed during initiation ceremonies when they took another step towards full membership of Ndebele society.

When the ear was slit, a few drops of blood fell onto the ground. In this way, the child made communion with her or his departed ancestors – the living dead. When a sufficiently large slit had been made, a piece of sorghum stalk was pushed into the hole. This stalk is called *isiqhazo*; its function was to prevent the hole closing up during the healing process.

"And was the man paid for this gruesome act?" I inquire from Gogo Matshazi. The answer is in the negative. However, the father of the child could, if he so wished, present a gift to the man in recognition of his invaluable services.

As the healing process continued, the child would turn *isiqhazo* in the slit hole. With further healing, *isiqhazo* would become loose and fall out, sometimes during sleep.

At times the hole deteriorated into a septic wound. Warm water was used to wash it. It was believed certain conditions led to the development of festering wounds. The man performing the ear cutting act should be spiritually clean. This entailed, among other things, abstaining from sexual activity. The underlying belief was that sex had a spiritually defiling effect.

When the children returned home, girls who had not reached puberty were expected to put spit into the slit to prevent it becoming septic. The belief was that menstruation was also a spiritually defiling condition that could inhibit the healing process.

Then I want to know what purpose, if any, was served by this painful process of slitting of ears.

"It was an identifying mark of a Ndebele person, an *uphawu*! If your ears are not cut, you don't hear properly, *uyisacuthe*," says Gogo Matshazi as she scratches her head.

"Is the practice still going on in Matabeleland?" I ask.

"Civilisation. The ways of the white man. It was thought the practice was unhygienic. Education and Christianity!" says Gogo Matshazi in a loud whisper that clearly acknowledges the power of western education and its formidable ally, Christianity.

In the Mzola area of Lupane, which is inhabited by the Makhandeni evictees of 1952, the practice only died out in the late 1970s when the liberation war escalated.

The millennium and the African concept of time

As we neared the year 2000, I received several inquiries about the Ndebele word for millennium. I gave the same answer on all occasions. "*Yimeleniyamu*, but remember, the Ndebele, like all other African peoples, did not have the concept of a millennium."

January 1, 2000 was significant in more ways than one. The day marked the start of a new year, 2000. More significantly, a new century, the twenty-first century, was ushered in. However, the greatest significance of the day lay in the fact that a new millennium, the third millennium, began.

Just what is a millennium and what is so special about it?

The Collins Dictionary gives the following definitions of millennium: 'the period of a thousand years of Christ's awaited reign upon earth', 'any period of one thousand years', 'a time of peace and happiness, especially in the distant future'.

The word millennium derives from two Latin words: 'mile', meaning a thousand and 'annus', meaning a year. Millennium, therefore, means a thousand years.

The basis of the millennium, indeed also that of the century, is to be found in the Gregorian Calendar based on Roman numerals which do not feature a zero. The base line – Jesus Christ's birth – is thus pegged at 1 AD, instead of 0 AD. Similarly, the years before his birth start with 1 BC.

This means, in effect, that the first millennium, that is, the thousand years after Christ's birth ran from January 1, 1 AD to December 1, 1000 AD. The first day of the second millennium was, therefore, January 1, 1001 AD. The third millennium, about which there was so much hype, only really started on January 1, 2001. The third millennium was celebrated one year too early. What matters though, is that there was agreement on the matter.

Why is this concept foreign to Africans? It is all to do with African thought regarding the concept of time.

"A noticeable feature of native life was the absence of any standards of measurement, such as time, distance, size, weight and so on. They had words for a day, moon, season of the year to indicate the passage of time. If asked when an event had taken place, the position of the sun, or moon, would be pointed out" (Thomas, undated).

Western thought conceptualises time as a linear concept with an infinite past, present and infinite future. African traditional thought differs markedly from this position. "For them (African people) time is simply a composition of events which have occurred, those which are taking place now and those which are immediately to occur" (Mbiti, 1969). Time has two dimensions, a long past and a short future (consisting of events that are occurring). Time has to be experienced in order to make sense or to become real. In other words, Africans concern themselves with the present and immediate future (referred to as *salsa* in KiSwahili) and an unlimited past (*ntolontolo*, as veteran writer Ndabezinhle Sigogo puts it, or *zamani* in KiSwahili).

It is this conceptualisation that makes Westerners say that Africans embrace 'no belief in progress'. There is no promise of a golden age in the future, no promise of a coming kingdom, or simply, no world to come as promised in Judaism and Christianity. Instead the golden age lies in the past that becomes an important reference point. The wise are the elders who were born earlier and are, therefore, nearer the source of wisdom.

Given this scenario, a millennium, being a period of a thousand years into the future, is beyond real time. Events occurring a thousand years from now are inconceivable. The millennium is, therefore, 'no-time' according to African thought. Time reckoning among Africans will illustrate this point further. Time is not reckoned for mathematical ends – hence no numerical calendars. Instead, time is reckoned for concrete and specific purposes. For example, cattle were an important component of the Ndebele economy. Reckoning of time of day made use of cattle. E*mpondo zankomo* is dawn, when sleeping cattle are only visible by their horns.

Lunar months are reckoned on the basis of weather conditions or other natural phenomena, for example *Zibandlela* (January) is the lunar month when paths, *izibandlela,* are covered (*ziba*) by growing grass. *Mpalakazi* (December) is the lunar month when impala mate.

The seasons of the year are similarly named. Among the Kalanga, summer is referred to as *hiha* - the time when food is plentiful in the fields and people's mouths are covered with remnants of what they have been eating (Interview with Adam Bango Dube, 1999).

Time is man centred. No human activity, no time. Africans can't be idle. When they engage in long, seemingly idle conversations, they are actually producing time for waiting for time.

Have you heard it said there is no hurry in Africa? I hope now you understand why!

Why a cattle kraal is sacred

The *Sunday News* of February 6, 2000 carried a story on the sacred dung scandal that rocked the tiny Swazi Kingdom. The scandal concerned the alleged theft of cow dung from the royal kraal by Parliamentary Speaker Mgabhi Dlamini. Apparently, the alleged theft of cow dung took place during the *Inxwala* (*Incwala* in Swazi) ceremony.

Stealing cow dung from the royal kraal is bad enough, but doing so during the *Inxwala* aggravates the crime. The ceremony is considered a key element in the beliefs and rituals that define and bind the nation. Rituals are performed to cleanse the kingship of the past year's misfortunes and strengthen its powers. The theft may seem harmless in some societies, but it certainly is not among traditional Africans where belief in witchcraft is still very strong.

"He obviously thinks that cooking cow dung will make him likeable to the King, and possibly to be made a minister," charged the Peoples United Democratic Movement.

Apparently, Speaker Mgabhi Dlamini maintains his act was done in good faith following a dream. Obtaining dung from the royal kraal was motivated by the desire to protect the royal family.

King Mswati III was not amused. The monarch did not wish to see the alleged cow dung thief again.

In order to fully appreciate the gravity of the situation one needs to understand a bit of pertinent traditional African religious philosophy. The cattle kraal symbolises the meeting point between the visible and invisible worlds. The family head communes with the departed ancestors in the cattle byre. In this regard, the cattle kraal becomes a holy place, a sacred shrine deserving of all reverence. This sacredness is brought about by cattle that have both economic and ritual value.

"Cattle are not only the link between the ancestors and their living descendents, but are the only means whereby the Zulu can at will get into touch with the ancestral spirits to make known his wants, or ask for blessing" (Krige, 1977).

In the case of the royal byre, the sacredness takes on national proportions, the royal byre being the spiritual nerve centre of the entire nation.

During *Inxwala*, royal cattle, called *amamvubu* in the case of the Ndebele, are ritually slaughtered. The meat is eaten by thousands of people gathered at the royal residence to take part in the national rejuvenation festivities.

It ought to be appreciated that cattle had important economic and social value in the traditional life of the Ndebele. Shields, *izihlangu*, for soldiers were made from hides. Women's dresses, *izidwaba*, were prepared from tanned leather. Furthermore, cattle were used as items of exchange to contract a marriage. A man with a large herd of cattle could acquire more wives for both himself and his sons.

No wonder, therefore, that the cattle kraal came to be associated with some important rituals such as *Inxwala*. When a bride left her parent's home, she went through the cattle byre. There, her father, through the use of frothing medicines, *isithundu*, informed the departed ancestors about one of their progeny who was leaving the family. *Isithundu* was also meant to make her become a cut above the rest of her husband's wives.

A place as sacred and important as the cattle kraal was invariably fortified, *ukubethelwa*, against witches.

"It is believed that a witch uses incantation, words, rituals and magic objects to inflict harm on her victims. To do this she may use the nails, hair, clothes or other possessions of the victims which she burns, pricks or wishes evil to" (Mbiti, 1991).

Among the Ndebele of Zimbabwe, there is a Khumalo house that is referred to as *'ababiya wenkosi'* or *'ababhoda umuzi wenkosi ngotsheko'*. Literally, this means those who fenced the royal residence with faeces. In reality, this is a reference to their role in fortifying the royal residence.

Witches approaching the royal town at night would see huge mounds of faeces. The king's residence, through the use of *umuthi*, appeared, at least in the eyes of the witches, like faeces.

The belief is that any royal item - clothing, parts of the body, excreta, indeed any item around the royal residence - carries some royal 'shadow', *ithunzi*. If people get hold of such items they can either harm the king, and hence the nation, or use these items to endear themselves to the king.

An example will illustrate this point. At Mhlahlandlela, King Mzilikazi Khumalo's last capital town, there used to be an *indaba* tree. Several people, particularly *izi-nyanga*, extracted bark from the tree (*umgugudu*). This was done in the belief that some of the 'Mzilikazi magic' would rub off onto them.

A story is told of how King Mzilikazi Khumalo overpowered Chief Magodonga Mahlangu, of the amaNzuza. The former's *inyanga*, Mphubane Mzizi, obtained a portion of the latter's faeces that he worked upon to effect the defeat of Magodonga (Mahlangu, 1957).

During ceremonies such as *Inxwala*, bones from slaughtered beasts were carefully collected to avoid them being smuggled out of the royal residence. The king later personally supervised the burning of the bones. All this and more was done to prevent theft of items that bore the royal shadow.

Indeed, recent archaeological research at Old Bulawayo unearthed several burnt bones within the Royal Enclosure. By comparison, there were fewer burnt bones in the Peripheral Settlement.

Stealing cow dung from the royal byre is without doubt a treasonable offence, for, in the hands of malevolent men, the dung could be worked upon magically with dire consequences to the very stability and continued existence of the kingdom.

The furore over the royal cow dung should be understood against practices whose effects have far reaching consequences on several aspects of national life. King Mswati III may literally and figuratively slip over the stolen cow dung.

No king, worth his royal mantle, will take these faecal machinations lying down.

The myths surrounding multiple births

Multiple births - be they twins, triplets or quadruplets – have traditionally caused alarm and apprehension among African societies. Several myths and practices relate to twins, known as *amaphahla* or *amawele* in Ndebele and *mapatya* in Shona. Twins used to face similar prejudices and misconceptions to albinos (*inkawu/masope*), physically challenged children and those who cut the upper teeth first.

"It was sometimes possible for a woman expecting twins to know about her condition. A sort of shallow linear depression would be visible on her womb," says Gogo Emma Matshazi.

This was the case before the twins turned to have their heads towards the birth canal. Babies that were born feet first were named Fulatha or Nyovane among the Ndebele. King Lobengula Khumalo's mother, Fulatha Tshabalala, was born in this manner.

The seniority of the twins was very important, determining inheritance and succession. It was believed that the twin who was born first was younger and the twin who was born second was older. It is difficult to understand why this was so. Perhaps the younger twin was faster and thus came out first. The elder twin, possessing less energy, was last to emerge. This thinking fits in with the seniority of the ancestors and the order in which they take possession of a spirit medium. The younger ancestors take possession of the medium first. The more senior seizes the medium last. During a traditional dance, this could very well be in the early hours of the morning.

A drama screened recently by the South African Broadcasting Corporation was based on the seniority of twins. The series was entitled '*Ityala lamawele*'. The twin who emerged first had his small finger cut off. That twin, however, receded into the womb. The second twin then came out first. Which one was the senior?

"Twins were regarded as abnormal, something unnatural. They were seen as a curse, some sort of bad luck," says Emmanuel Mugomba.

The belief was that twins were not ordinary. In some African societies they were considered to have no brains or to be unusually sharp and clever. Others even suggested that twins possessed special powers from God.

Beliefs that people hold influence their attitudes and hence their behaviour. Beating twins was thought to bring bad luck to the perpetrator. Beating a twin was like beating a spirit, *ithongo*. Where twins were thought to possess special powers, they were asked to settle squabbles or to foretell the weather.

However, those societies who saw twins as some kind of misfortune conducted ceremonies to prevent misfortune happening again. In such societies twins "... were experienced as a threat to their whole existence, as a sign that something wrong had happened to cause the births and that something worse still would happen to the whole community if the 'evil' were not removed. So they killed the children for the sake of the larger community, to cleanse, to 'save' or protect the rest of the people" (Mbiti, 1969).

"The midwife was empowered to kill the twins. The matter was not announced to the family. Old women buried the dead twins quietly on the river bank. The grave was not to be identified. When community members asked about the fate of her pregnancy, the response would be '*Aiwa wakatadza*' ('She failed')," says Emmanuel Mugomba.

A similar fate seems to have greeted twins among the Zulu of South Africa. One of them was killed by having a lump of earth placed in its throat. If this was not done, the belief was that someone else in the family would die (Krige, 1977).

Among the Ndebele the terminology used in reference to twins was also different. People never said a twin was ill. They would say 'it is a cry-baby', '*kuyadedesa*', or 'it is proud', '*kuyimbudlwana*' or '*kuyazigqaja*'.

When a twin fell ill, he or she was not given herbs. "Its mother took it to the ash midden (*isilotha*) beyond the palisade and abandoned it briefly. Someone else would go to pick it up," says Gogo Emma Matshazi. The ash treatment suggests some unnatural attributes of twins. "When a twin boy is troublesome, they simply put ashes on the nape of his neck and give him some ashes and water to drink" (Krige, 1977). A trip to talk at the ash midden was also used to normalise relations between two feuding men, *ukukhumelana umlotha* ('licking the ash').

Another treatment for twins was incense called *imphepha*. The incense was burnt and the twin made to inhale the smoke, or his or her mother would rub *imphepha* onto the twin's body to 'wash it', *akutshubaqe, akugezise.*

Impepha is often used by spirit mediums. The smoke has an aroma that is good to the nostrils of the ancestors. The use of *imphepha* on a twin may suggest some supernatural powers by the twins.

A hot tempered twin is referred to as *iscaphucaphu,* an extremely quiet twin is *impuza.*

Twins' behaviour has been used to chastise other children. A mother may say to her children '*munoitireyi zvakadaro, asimurimapatya?*' (Why do you behave like twins?).

When one twin died, special terminology was used. If a boy died, he was said to have gone to herd cattle, *kuyekwelusa*. In the case of a girl, it was said she had got married, *ukuyayenda*. In both cases there was no wailing, as would be the case with other children. It was thought the surviving twin would die from shock.

There were two options when it came to burial arrangements. One option was that the grave was dug and the surviving twin was placed in the open grave. He or she was later removed and the corpse of the deceased twin was laid to rest. Sometimes the corpse was made to hold a wooden log.

Alternatively, the corpse was buried and the surviving twin was made to wash on the covered grave of the deceased twin. In both cases the idea seems to have been to convince the departed spirit that its companion was accompanying it to the spirit world just as when they occupied the same womb at the same time. Together in the womb, together in the grave and together in the spirit world – this seems to have been the underlying principle.

People of Godlwayo retain identity and pride

Maduna Mafu, the chief of Godlwayo, led the armed struggle of 1896 in the eastern Ndebele State, together with other leaders such as Mahlahleni Mafu, Siminzela Mathema and Fezela Khumalo.

Godlwayo was formed during the time when the Ndebele were resident in the present day Pretoria area. King Mzilikazi Khumalo was domiciled at Mhlahlandlela, his capital located near present day Hammanskral.

The first chief of Godlwayo was Dambisamahubo Mafu. The village was also called Dambisamahubo Mafu and was associated with Amnyama Angankomo, whose main village was Umzinyathini under Chief Majijili Gwebu.

Godlwayo would have started as a military unit which, when its members married, transformed into a village, *umuzi*. Young men, from the same age group, were conscripted into a new unit, which was given a heroic name and a chief appointed over it. Esprit de corps developed among the unit personnel. Heroic praises were formulated which members of Godlwayo would proudly recite.

Ugodlway' omnyama
Umahlab' ayitwale
Umakhahlela nyovane njengesibhamu samaKhiwa
Amafela ndawonye.
Abaphumbul' injanji yezitimela ngobolo.

One more example of praises for an *umuzi* will suffice. These refer to Insukamini, whose chief was Manondwana Tshabalala.

Insukamini
Ibhinda litshone
Umdl' adlule njenngentethe
Insukamini eyakhela umkhaya!
(as given by Nijo Lusinga in Nyathi (2000))

Each unit, or *ibutho*, composed a song for itself. The men carried shields of the same colour and all this added to the distinct identity of that unit.
In Zimbabwe, Godlwayo, as part of Amnyama Angankomo, settled north of the confluence of the Ncema and Mzingwane rivers.

Dambisamahubo Mafu is said to have escaped death when some chiefs, accused of installing Nkulumane in the absence of King Mzilikazi Khumalo, were tried and found guilty of treason.

His son, Mthikana, succeeded him and was later killed on the instruction of King Lobengula Khumalo. He was accused of supporting Nkulumane during the civil war of 1871-72. Mthikana, who owned a horse in the 1870s, was a rich man. Royal princesses were privileged to nominate a husband of their choice. Invariably, they chose rich men, most of whom were chiefs. It was a crime to turn down such a proposition. King Mzilikazi's daughter, Makhwa, chose Mthikana as her husband.

King Mzilikazi Khumalo (he had no less than 300 wives) came to possess several herds of cattle through his daughters marrying rich men. For example, Mehlomakhulu Dlodlo, Chief of Emakhandeni, paid a hundred head of cattle for Bitshi, King Mzilikazi Khumalo's daughter by Loziba Thebe (okaPhahlana), the chief queen who lived at Emhlangeni (Inyathi).

Makhwa, by virtue of being a royal princess, took precedence over Mthikana's older wives. Her eldest son, Maduna, succeeded Mthikana as chief of Godlwayo. This is the man who led Godlwayo during Imfazo II in 1896. Subsequently, Maduna fled to Mberengwa (Emphatheni) and was thus not among the Ndebele chiefs who met with Cecil John Rhodes in the Matopos to hammer out a peace deal.

At the time of Imfazo II, Godlwayo, whose population comprised the Nguni from Zululand, Shona/Kalanga incorporates, the Sotho and Venda of Tshivhasa (Sibasa), was located near the Shazhabuhwa Mountain.

The only state witness due to appear in the trial of Chief Maduna after Imfazo II was a white man. The day before he was to testify against Chief Maduna, a bolt of lightning struck him, killing him instantly. With the sole state witness dead, Chief Maduna was acquitted. That is how he escaped certain death. He then became a salaried chief under colonial administration.

Jim Nduna Mafu assumed the reins of power following the death of Maduna, succeeded by Vezi Maduna Mafu, who is the reigning chief of Godlwayo.

What is of particular interest, though, is that of all former Ndebele *imizi*, Godlwayo stands head and shoulders above them all in having successfully retained its pride and identity to this day.

Several reasons can be advanced to explain this. Following colonisation, the Ndebele people suffered land alienation and accompanying evictions more than any other African group in Zimbabwe. People belonging to the same village were scattered and found themselves belonging to several villages far away from their original ancestral homes. For example, the people of Intemba, once under Xukuthwayo Mlotshwa and later Sikhombo Mguni, went to Jambezi Entunteni, Matshethseni and Ntabazinduna. Their chieftainship, now taken over by Xukuthwayo's son Mvuthu, was resuscitated in Jambezi, although most of his followers were not originally of Entembeni, having been evicted from various areas such as Silobela and Matopo.

By and large, the Godlwayo people were not similarly scattered. The majority of them are today found in the area referred to as koGodlwayo.

The colonial administration dissolved certain chieftainships, especially where the chiefs concerned were regarded as rebels. Inzwananzi, Imbizo, Inyanda and Insukamini are among several *imizi* whose chieftainships were discontinued.

It was not so with Godlwayo, which has, since about the early 1830s, always been under the Mafus. The present chief, Vezi Maduna Mafu, is a descendant of the founding chief of Godlwayo, Dambisamahubo.

During the colonial era, some chiefs became willing agents of the white regime. With the rise of nationalism, especially in the 60s, some of them were discredited or even killed. This was not so with the Chief of Godlwayo, Vezi Maduna, who was a dedicated leader of ZAPU. During the height of the liberation struggle, Chief Vezi Maduna was arrested. '"Chief Maduna, you are under arrest in term of section twelve subsection four of the Law and Order Maintenance Act, chapter sixty–five", said Inspector Buxton, leaning out of his Land Rover window' (Godwin, 1996).

Vezi Maduna spent the rest of the war in Whawha Prison. The man who was elevated to the position of chief during Vezi Maduna's imprisonment was ignored by the people of Godlwayo. Vezi Maduna's credibility lies in the fact that he stood with his people through thick and thin.

Perhaps as a result of the reasons given above, the people of Godlwayo are conscious of their history. It is not uncommon to hear men and women in towns addressing each other as 'Egodlwayo'. For some men, Godlwayo has become their name. Others have their homesteads or farms referred to as Godlwayo. Further, the consciousness transcends all levels of formal education. An *imbube* group, Bright Star Godlwayo Omnyama, continues to perpetuate that identity.

After the political colonisation of Zimbabwe, various church denominations followed suit with their brand of colonisation. A denomination in a particular area would tend to elbow out competing denominations. Only in a few areas did several denominations co-exist.

In the Godlwayo area, the predominant denomination was the Brethren in Christ Church, which set up its missions at Matopo (1898), Mtshabezi and Wanezi. The church further consolidated the historical and geographical ties among the people. Churches provided health and educational services over and above their core business of evangelising the 'heathens' (*abahedeni*). The Brethren in Christ Church opened up both primary and secondary schools within its sphere of influence. Often, students, on completing their courses, went to live in town. There, they continued to attend church services in the urban Brethren in Christ Church. On a social level, they continued to interact as former school mates, home boys or home girls. The net result of all this is the perpetuation of the identity of Godlwayo. Inqama, in the Gwanda district, would probably come second after Godlwayo, for reasons similar to those enumerated above.

Witchcraft

"This belief (in witchcraft) is found in all African societies," claims John Mbiti (1991). Witchcraft was so much an integral part of traditional Africa that some early whites regarded it as synonymous with African religion.

Where the hunted don't write, their own history shall be told by the hunters. It is so with witchcraft. By virtue of its nature and mode of operation, its intricacies remain shrouded in the mists of conjecture and prejudice. Witchcraft operates from the premise that there is an energy in the world which knowledgeable men and women can harness to produce desired effects.

Mbiti (1991) defines witchcraft as a manifestation of mystical forces that may be inherent in a person, or acquired in various ways. Krige (1977) states that witchcraft is due to the working of unseen forces. Detection of witchcraft will not take place until its nature is fully comprehended.

Witchcraft is said to be fuelled by hatred, jealousy, envy and a deep sense of malice. Hardly ever is it used against strangers with whom the witch/wizard has no social interaction, but more often against neighbours and relatives.

Some people are born witches, some acquire the skills of witchcraft, and yet others have witchcraft thrust upon them. In interview George Moyo (2000) confides that people possessed by an evil spirit have the potential to become witches, they only need to be initiated by accomplished witches. Initiation involves eating human flesh mixed with herbs. The most dangerous witches are those who are possessed by an evil spirit.

The belief is that a witch can also be initiated through medicine inserted into incisions made on the backbone, one toe and one finger. As the *uhlanga* (incision) matures, the medium acquires the skills of witchcraft.

In another instance, a man or woman may acquire the requisite knowledge about herbs and use it to harm foes or competitors.

The dynamism of African religion lies in the contradictory forces of good and bad. Witchcraft represents the bad side, which the good spirits - as represented by the traditional doctors – are constantly fighting. In the absence of witchcraft, probably more than 70 percent of traditional healing would be rendered irrelevant.

There are thought to be various ways in which witches attack their victims. Harmful objects may be dug into the ground or across the path of the intended victim. Creatures like bees, moths and bats may be sent to the targeted victim. Incantations or words may be used to bring about evil results.

It is commonly believed that witches make use of familiars in their evil errands. "Every *umthakathi* (witch/wizard) has his familiars who help him in his evil work and obey his commands" (Krige, 1977). Familiars range from wild animals, domestic animals, birds, insects and snakes to human beings. The witches' companions serve as means of transport and agents of evil machinations.

Most African peoples in Southern Africa regard the antbear, *isambana bikita/wombela*, as the most commonly used mode of transport. It is claimed that witches use a skin placed on the powerful animal into which they shove their bent knees. The antbear and its rider face in the same direction. Quite often the antbear is liberally festooned with beads of various colours. The antbear, a fast digger, is thought to be used to retrieve corpses from graves. It may start digging from kilometres away in order to reach the corpse. On the surface, the grave will look undisturbed.

Another animal that is often thought to be used as a means of transport is the baboon. In this case, however, the rider sits backwards while the baboon, its neck supporting the rider's legs, leads the way.

It seems that a human being, *isothamlilo,* is another convenient means of transport, walking with the witch riding like a baby. Quite often, the person is not aware of the fact that he/she is used on nocturnal errands.

The hyena is another animal said to be used as a means of transport. It has powerful muscles capable of lifting a well fed witch.

The donkey is also considered a familiar that provides dependable transport. Its strong back can carry more than one witch at a time. Witches, it seems, are capable of transforming themselves into donkeys. If one sees several donkeys at one's home, they could be witches disguised as beasts of burden.

Other types of familiar are used to cause illness or death. Their sighting within a homestead could foretell evil.

"Indeed, *abathakathi* are in league with all kinds of birds and animals, and when an owl hoots near a hut, it is believed to forebode evil or death, because it's the messenger of some *umthakathi*" (Krige, 1977).

Umkhoba is feared by many as it is believed to beat up its victims, who display signs and symptoms akin to those of a victim of a stroke. The little creature is made in various ways, including the use of clay mixed with herbs and human blood.

Umatholwane or *undofa* share some traits with *umkhoba*. In this instance, the victim is made to disappear. The little creature is invisible. The tip of the tongue is also cut off so that it does not speak clearly. Stories about *undofa* abound. It is alleged that some are kept in shebeens where they participate in night long parties. "*Kuthe kuthe!*" they have been heard to shout, meaning "*kuze kuse*" (all night long) (Interview with George Moyo, 2000).

Dogs, it is said, can also be used as familiars. A dog on such an evil mission is seen after midnight, often in the company of other dogs. It is, however, bigger than the rest of the dogs. It whines in a strange way, *ukuhlaba umkhulungwane.*

Other animals falling into this category include *impunzi* (duiker), *iqaqa* (civet cat) and *ululwane* (bat).

A bird that is feared is the owl, *ugweru. Impundulu,* commonly feared in South Africa, is made from parts of a bat, part of an ostrich's foot and some herbs. The creature appears as a bat and gives a fatal ostrich kick.

Among snakes, *umgobho* is the most feared. The huge snake, with a crown on its head, strikes victims on their head. As a precaution, people carry stones on their heads when they pass through an area said to have the colossal snake which cries like a goat.

Some familiars, like *ondofa* and *umgobho,* are believed to do work for their witches. Tasks performed include herding cattle, watering crops and stealing goods.

When witches go on their nocturnal errands, what happens to their spouses? An animal, such as *impunzi* or *ingiga*, is thought to be placed next to the sleeping partner. The animal may be covered in human skin (*isikhumba sesothamlilo).* The spouse then believes that his/her partner is sleeping beside her/him.

Witchcraft may have some social benefits. Fear of being bewitched might discourage people from engaging in anti-social activities.

Belief in afterlife shown in burial methods

By now the night is pitch black. For a while I am oblivious to the comfort of our Mercedes Benz. I still have interviews to conduct. I shudder to think what time we will get back to Bulawayo.

Earlier on, what I had initially taken to be stars turned out to be Dadaya High School lights. This is Sir Garfield Todd's territory. The missionary turned politician taught many boys who later became leading nationalists and academics.

At Gwatemba small scale farming area we turn off into a farm. The Morris Carter Commission, set up in 1925, recommended the segregation of land. Its recommendations were translated into the Land Apportionment Act of 1930. The Act created Native Purchase Areas where Africans could buy and own land on a freehold basis. The colonists hoped to create buffer zones between their farms and the native reserves. Gwatemba is one former Native Purchase Area.

As soon as our car lights up the homestead, the occupants wake from their slumber and stream out of their houses to give us a warm African welcome. We all assemble in the open space next to the main house. We use torches and car lights to keep the darkness at bay. In order not to run down the car battery, the engine is left running.

Quickly, I get out pen and paper, the tools of my trade. During interviews such as this one, I get information relating to the project at hand. At the same time I obtain information not directly relevant to my research, but which is useful historical information that should not be allowed to pass into oblivion. My informant, Mlotshwa, born in 1906, has an excellent memory and is a veritable mine of historical information. He originally came from Intemba Village under Sikhombo Mguni. Intembeni people were evicted shortly after the 1918 influenza epidemic. They were pushed to the Malungwana area. Prior to their eviction, they lived in the area stretching from Heany Junction to the Ncema River. Their chief was Xukuthwayo Mlotshwa, King Lobengula Khumalo's eminent poet.

Intemba village consisted of dispersed sub-villages of varying sizes. Some were small, but the vast majority were large. Generally, a number of related men lived together. Usually a village was known by the name of the head of the household.

On his death, the head of the household was buried next to the cattle pen. In a big sub-village, the rest of the men were not buried next to the cattle kraal, but often out of the village, preferably on ant hills.

In those days, bodies were buried in the squatting position. On dying, a man had his arms and legs folded. This is why the Ndebele will say, about one who has died, "*Uye kogoqanyawo*" or "*uye kosonganyawana*".

One of Mlotshwa's sons is sitting attentively next to his mother. The history that his father is explaining is not known to him. This interview has provided him with a golden opportunity to learn of his people's history.

The positioning of the dead body is all to do with war preparedness. It is quicker and easier to stand up and defend oneself from a squatting position than it is from a sleeping one. The belief is that there is life beyond the grave. Life on that plane of existence is very similar to this one. A soldier on earth is a soldier in the hereafter. Besides, I think to myself, the method saves space.

One question I forgot to ask, "Were women also buried in this squatting position?" In life they did not squat. I wonder if they will do so in life after death. I need to go back to Gwatemba to clarify this.

Before colonisation, Chief Xhukuthwayo Mlotshwa died. The question of succession, ever a grey issue among the Ndebele people, loomed large. There was a special relationship between the King and the senior chiefs. The King married a chief's daughter while a chief married a king's daughter.

Xhukuthwayo Mlotshwa married Mzilikazi's granddaughter, uLodumba. Her father was Qhalingana and her brother was Sikonkwane Khumalo. Their eldest son was Debe. It was hoped that Debe would become Chief, following the death of his father.

Later, Xhukuthwayo married Mzilikazi's daughter. Their son was Mvuthu. Who, between Debe and Mvuthu, was the heir to the chieftainship?

Mvuthu's mother, being a direct daughter of King Mzilikazi Khumalo, took precedence over Debe, whose mother was King Mzilikazi's granddaughter, a niece to Mvuthu's mother.

Because Mvuthu was still young, a regent was sought to lead the people of Entembeni. Sikhombo Mguni was chosen to be the caretaker of Intemba and Izinkondo zika Njojo villages.

When Cecil John Rhodes' emissaries came to seek a mining concession from King Lobengula Khumalo in 1888 (the Rudd Concession), Sikhombo Mguni was a prominent chief in the Ndebele State. It is alleged that Sikhombo Mguni, together with Inkosi yamaaNtshali Lotshe Hlabangana, was bribed by the emissaries (namely, Charles Dunnel Rudd, James Rochford Maguire, and Francis 'Matabele' Thompson). They prevailed over the King to sign the concession, which gave Rhodes mineral rights in exchange for guns, amongst other things. Lotshe, having been thoroughly beaten in battle by Ndawana/Tawana's warriors in the Lake Ngami area, knew how important it was for the Ndebele armies to acquire firearms.

Rituals and taboos surrounding death

Virtually all black African societies embraced belief in life beyond the grave. When someone died there were attendant rituals to prepare the passage of the spirit into the next world.

Terminology used to describe death bears testimony to the indestructibility of the spirit. Among the Ndebele, when someone has died, such expressions as the following are used: *usedlule* (she has passed on), *usethule* (he is silent/quiet), *usetshonile* (she has disappeared/set), *umoya usuphumile* (the spirit has left the body), *usechimezile* (he has closed his eyes), *usehambile* (she has moved on), *usephumule* (she has rested), *usephelile* (he is finished), *usechitshile* (she is extinguished/expired).

With regard to royalty more powerful images were used: i*nkosi sikhotheme* (the King has bowed), *ilanga selitshonile* (the sun has set) or *intaba* i*sidilikile* (the mountain has fallen).

When someone died, the spirit and the physical body separated. Members of the community performed various rituals to facilitate the smooth passage of the spirit into the next world. At the same time, measures were taken to minimise pain and shock among the surviving members.

Death, it was believed, defiles. Close relatives of the deceased had to be cleansed in order to rid themselves of the defilement. The same applied to implements that were used to dig the grave. In the past sharpened wooden sticks, *ingibho*, were used to dig the grave (Interview with Lot Mathiba Nyathi, 2000). Later, sharpened iron rods, *izimbo*, were used for digging. Hoes came next and have now been replaced by picks and spades. The ritual cleansing, known as *ukugezisa amakhuba* (cleansing of hoes) was performed a week or two after the funeral, depending on individual circumstances.

It is this belief in defilement that explains why the Ndebele kings did not want to be visited by the bereaved. It is recorded that one reason for the relocation of the Royal Town was the death of the chief queen. King Mzilikazi Khumalo moved from Emahlokohlokweni II following the death of an unnamed queen. A similar reason accounted for his movement from Emhlangeni (Inyathi) following the death of *unina womuzi*, Lozibaa Thebe (*OkaPhahlana*), who died in 1861, to his final capital town of Mhlahlandlela.

On the day of a burial, certain rituals were performed to cleanse the people who came into contact with the corpse. Those who had reason to view the corpse, such as the close relatives, had white medicine applied below each eye.

As soon as the body was buried, the hut in which it had lain was cleansed using *intelezi* medicines. The *inyanga* dipped his flywhisk, *itshoba*, in medicine and sprayed, *ukuchela*, the entire hut. While the corpse lay in the hut, ashes were not taken out of the village.

Following burial and the cleansing of the entire homestead, the *inyanga* lit a torch consisting of a dried twig smeared with medicine. He moved into the hut where the body had lain and moved about with his cleansing flame lifted high. Close relatives returning from the burial partook of cleansing medicinal concoctions, *ukuhabula ixolo*. The first sip was spat out and the second was swallowed. This was done outside the homestead and was meant to take care of internal cleansing.

External cleansing was achieved by taking a medicated bath. Medicines called *izintelezi* were mixed with water and defiled persons bathed their bodies.

Nowadays shortcuts are resorted to. At the entrance two dishes are placed for the returning mourners. One dish contains a single herb, usually *umsuzwane*, and people wash their hands and faces. The other dish of plain water is meant for people who have embraced foreign ideas.

The beast slaughtered on the day had its meat, called *ingovu*, eaten without salt. All the bones were collected and later burnt. Any meat uneaten was kept outside the homestead to be eaten by relatives who arrived late.

All these rituals were performed on the day of the burial. However, the cleansing process continued the next day. The next stage, known as *ukwehlisa abantu entabeni,* was reserved for close relatives only. The officiating *inyanga* made what is known as *ilumo.* This consisted of a mixture of all the grain available in the homestead. The grain and some herbs were ground together using a pestle and mortar. A little water was added in order to make a thick paste that was stuck on to a forked piece of stick.

Next the *inyanga* prepared two medicinal mixtures. The first consisted of burnt herbs used in *ilumo* plus milk fat, *iphehla.* These days Vaseline has replaced *iphehla.* The second consisted of herbs and milk. Armed with these herbal potions, the *inyanga* and his assistants requested all the close relatives to move to the cattle kraal. The *inyanga* and his lieutenants took their positions. The first assistant, using a crude brush made from a thin tree trunk, smeared the black paste onto the relatives filing past him. The paste was applied on the side of the relatives' bodies.

The *inyanga* was next in line. Each relative took a single bite of *ilumo*, which the *inyanga* was holding. The final stage was completed by the second assistant who was holding a piece of gourd filled with the mixture of herbs and milk. Each relative took a sip and spat this to the ground. The second sip was swallowed. Relatives took turns until they had all filed past.

Leaves from the plant used in the milk and Vaseline concoction were thrown around in and outside the cattle kraal. Death was thought to be so defiling that it caused cows to miscarry. Scattering of the leaves was meant to avert miscarriages among cows in calf.

Once these rituals had been performed, bereavement rituals, *ukuzila*, followed. Sexual intercourse was refrained from for a number of days, *ukuzila amacansi*. If the deceased was male, his wives cut off their hair including the top knot, *icholo*. The close relatives similarly cut off their hair. Wives generally washed little during this period. This, as well as the wearing of bereavement strips over their heads, *imicwazi*, warded off would be suitors. Wives remained in this state of mourning until the deceased's relatives conducted the bringing home ceremony, *umbuyiso*.

A week or so later more rituals were conducted to ease the burden on the bereaved and also to facilitate the safe passage of the departed spirit into the next world, *kwelamathongo*.

Sacred rituals observed during a matriarch's burial

My mother died on March 17, 2000 and I attended the ritual cleansing, *ukugesiza amakhuba*, on April 8 at Sankonjana

Close relatives gathered in the hut where the beer brewed for the occasion was placed. The men, mostly Nyathis, sat on the side of the hut, *isilili sesilisa* (the right side as one stands facing the hut). The women sat on the female side, *isilili sesifazana*.

"*Sitshengiseni uutshwala bempisi,*" demanded my father, Menyezwa. Literally, he meant beer for the hyenas - the two men who had placed the corpse in the grave. Because these men, 'hyenas', were the most defiled, they enjoyed favoured status. The two women who had brewed the beer pointed at one calabash frothing at its mouth. This was the calabash set aside for the 'hyenas', to dispose of as they saw fit. They could, on their own, do justice to the beer. Alternatively, they could share it with other people. The latter was the case.

My father, in his capacity as medicine man and chief of protocol, took a little beer, *insipho*, and *ingwebu* and mixed them. He smeared the faces of the 'hyenas'. This was followed by the sprinkling of all the people gathered in the hut, *ukuchela*. A fly whisk, *itshoba*, was used. Aunt Mthethephi Nyathi carried a small beer calabash, expertly balanced on her head, and led the procession to the grave, some distance from the homestead.

Normally, women are buried at the rear of the homesteads – next to the granaries that house the products of their labour. Before the advent of Blair toilets, this was the area where women went to answer the call of nature. On this occasion, the granary area was waterlogged following the heavy rains induced by Cyclone Eline and so an anthill had been chosen.

In the past, men went to the front of the homestead to empty their bladders. The head of a household was buried next to the cattle fold, which was always in front of the village.

The word, spoken or silent, is the key to communicating with the departed spirits. That responsibility fell on my father. He drank a little, *ukucabula*, from the beer calabash and spat on the ground. He repeated the procedure, this time swallowing the beer. The calabash was passed around and the same procedure was performed by all present. The little beer remaining was poured on the ground. The empty calabash was then placed on the grave covered in stones, *intaba*, and *umphafa / umlahlabantu* tree branches.

Relatives then had the opportunity to address the departed spirit, probably the first time since the separation of body and spirit.

Following this the mourners streamed back home. The next stage involved the cleansing of implements used during the digging of the grave. Using cleansing herbs, *amakhambi okuchela*, and a bit of beer, my father sprinkled these.

Meanwhile, items of clothing and utensils had been piled up in front of the kitchen hut. Next to these was another cleansing mixture. Relatives dipped their hands into the mixture and touched all the items. This ritual is known as *ukubamba impahla*.

Items of clothing were gathered in one place to await yet another ritual – *ukuchitha impahla*, the distribution of the deceased's clothing.

THE XHOSA (AMAFENGU)

The amaFengu of Zimbabwe constitute a small community that has been in Zimbabwe for over 100 years. The term Fengu, or Fingo, is derived from the word *ukufenguza*, which means to beg or to ask for a place to settle. The term is not accepted by the people concerned. They prefer to be called Xhosa. Indeed, their language and cultural practices are Xhosa.

Originally, the Zimbabwean Xhosa belonged to the Hlubi ethnic group in what is today KwaZulu-Natal. Many of them were Dlaminis, Hadebe and Kuboni. The upheavals of the first quarter of the nineteenth century, also known as *Mfecane*, led to their dispersal. They subsequently sought refuge among the Xhosa in the south, hence the name amaFengu. Over a period of time, they became acculturated. They embraced the Xhosa language and cultural practices.

Various processes were at work leading to the introduction of the Xhosa into Zimbabwe. Following the occupation of Matabeleland in 1893, the Ndebele took up arms in 1896 in an effort to re-establish the erstwhile Ndebele State. In that military campaign Cecil Rhodes made use of Xhosa men, derogatively known as Cape Boys.

Rhodes viewed the Ndebele as a warlike people who needed to be neutralised through the introduction into Matabeleland of Christians from South Africa. For a start, he encouraged missionaries to settle in the hills so that they could "build up groups of African Christians responsive both to development and discipline" (Ranger, 1999). The Brethren in Christ Church was allowed to set up Matopo Mission in 1898. The Anglicans were eventually allowed into the mountains to establish Cyrene Mission.

The Ngwato chief Raditladi made an application to settle within the Matopo Hills. While Cecil John Rhodes was favourable to the idea, the British High Commissioner Milner shot it down.

In May 1898 Cecil John Rhodes put together a scheme to import 'loyal and progressive' Mfengu from the Cape. After all, many so-called Cape Boys, like John Grootboom, fought alongside the whites in 1896. Rhodes promised the Mfengu three 'reserves' on which they could settle with the proviso that each man would work for three months every year. After 36 months of labour each one of them would be given an individual title, *amatatitele*, to five morgen of land (Ranger, 1999). Though Rhodes' scheme did not materialise in the Matopo Hills, it did with regards to Mbembesi where the Mfengu were introduced. They came by train via Mafikeng.

The Ndebele responded by seeking legal advice from a white lawyer to halt the impending immigration. The Ndebele also considered sending a delegation to the British Queen with the express purpose of halting the planned importation and also to demand the restoration of the Ndebele monarchy. But, in the end, no action was taken.

The Xhosa immigrants lived apart from the Ndebele community. That way they preserved their cultural practices and their language has survived to this day. In 2000 the Mbembesi Xhosa community celebrated the centenary of their arrival in Zimbabwe.

Some Xhosa, and indeed, other Africans, came to Southern Rhodesia as clergymen in the service of their Christian denominations, such as Wesleyan Methodists, Salvationists, Anglicans, Presbyterians and Lutherans.

As far back as the second half of the nineteenth century, black people from Zimbabwe went to South Africa to work in the diamond mines in Kimberley and the gold mines in the Witwatersrand. After colonisation the practice continued. Some of the Zimbabwean migrants married Xhosa women who then came to live in Zimbabwe with their husbands.

Some South African blacks, who received western education much earlier than their Zimbabwean counterparts, trained as teachers and nurses and came to work in Zimbabwe. In most cases they were allied to the various churches that operated in Zimbabwe. There was another group of Xhosa who came to Zimbabwe as drivers of ox-wagons plying the route between Zimbabwe and South Africa.

While most of the Xhosa community in Zimbabwe was to be found in the Mbembesi area, there were others scattered in various parts of Zimbabwe such as Makwiro, Chitomborwizi, Musengezi and Marirangwe. Some of them bought agricultural plots in the Native Purchase Areas.

Some members of the Xhosa community came to play an important role in nationalism and the armed liberation struggle that culminated in Zimbabwe's independence in 1980.

In the post independence era, when resettlement was embarked upon, some Xhosa left their Mbembesi homeland to live in newly acquired land. Some of these are now found in areas such as Kennilworth, Circle C and Insiza. However, resettlement was not exclusive to the Xhosa. They now live side by side with Ndebele people. The new pattern of settlement may dilute or even threaten Xhosa culture that hitherto has held its own in the face of the more dominant cultures of its neighbours.

Male circumcision among the amaXhosa of Zimbabwe

The amaFengu of Mbembesi, north-east of Bulawayo, are a cultural curiosity in Matabeleland. They are the only ethnic group that practices male circumcision.

The amaFengu are a heterogeneous people comprising several ethnic groups, such as the Hlubi amaBhele, amaNtambo, amaZizi and amaTolo.

During the times of *Mfecane* they fled Zululand where nation was turning against nation. Matiwane of the Ngwane people set upon the Hlubi of Chief Mpangazitha who fled westwards, while some of the Hlubi struck southwards towards Xhosaland.

After Mpangazitha's death, those that went westwards were led by Mehlomakhulu. It was Mehlomakhulu who, with his followers, joined the Ndebele of Mzilikazi Khumalo in 1826 on the Likhwa (Vaal) River. This was the first Ndebele settlement called koMkhwahla. The Dlodlos in Zimbabwe are descendants of Mpangazitha.

One custom that the Mfengu acquired from the Xhosa was male circumcision, *ukwelusa amakhwenkwe* (singular - *inkwenkwe).*

Just before the circumcision ceremony, *umguyo*, is performed, an *inkwenkwe* takes part in a ceremony called *ingxelo* during which he announces to relatives his intention to undergo circumcision. The boy sings the song '*Sendingayimela, Sendingayimela*' (Interview with Felicity Gangada, 1999).

Amakhwenkwe leave their homes to live in a special hut, called *ibhoma,* where they are secluded for the duration of the ceremony. In the past, *ibhoma* (the name is thought to derive from an Arabic word) was a beehive hut. These days in South Africa a plastic shack will pass for *ibhoma*. In Zimbabwe, tree branches and grass are used, as these are still plentiful.

Amakhwenkwe discard their old clothes and wrap a blanket around themselves. They apply *inguke,* a white limestone powder, on their faces meant to serve as a warning to all and sundry so that they avoid the initiates, *abakhwetha.*

The services of a specialist at cutting the foreskin are sought. This specialist is called *ingcibi* (Interview with Reverend Father Elliot Dhlula, 1999). The specialist uses a sharp spear, *umkhonto,* a razor or a special knife. To achieve a keen blade, these instruments are sharpened on a piece of leather.

Great significance is attached to the blood spilt during the circumcision, *ukuchitha igazi*. The spilling of blood onto the soil is a sacrifice, which means that the initiated person is hence forward bound "to the land and consequently to the departed members of his society. It says that the individual is alive and that he now wishes to be tied to the community and people among whom he has been born as a child. The circumcision blood is like making a covenant, or a solemn agreement between the individual and his people. Until the individual has gone through the operation, he is still an outsider. Once he joins the stream of his people, he becomes truly one with them" (Ramose, 1980). *Isiqgutsi*, some softened up leaves, are used to dress the wound. A soft goat skin, with hairs removed, is wrapped around the leaves. This soft skin is called *ityeba* (Interview with Reverend Father Elliot Dhlula, 1999).

For the first seven days, initiates, who are looked after by *ikhankatha* – a sort of nursing and cultural adviser - are not allowed to drink water. Possibly this serves to minimise the frequent emptying of one's bladder. Passing urine would be painful. Similarly, if the penis became erect, the initiate would feel intense pain. The solution is to sjambok the initiate. When he feels the sjambok pain, the erection subsides and the pain from the circumcision is eased. Pain stops pain.

Abakhwetha then go to the river to symbolically wash away their youthfulness. *Ibhoma* is set on fire after the ceremony. The initiates are not allowed to look back. They leave behind a stage that is symbolised by the burning *ibhoma*.

If girls wish to visit the initiates they are required to announce their presence from afar. Girls may take presents to give to the initiates. These are usually tobacco, *icuba*, or even sweets, depending on the taste of the initiate.

For a year after the ceremony, the young man is known as *ikrala (iklwala)*. Now, and only now, is he a man who is fully integrated into society. He is incorporated into the community of the living dead, and, above all, he is qualified to marry.

Now he is accountable for his actions. Before then, he was regarded as *inkwenkwe,* and it is said *inkwenkwe yinja.* This, in essence, means his misdemeanours were tolerated. Not so when he has become a man!

Society expects him to get married and raise children. Marriage, according to African belief, links the departed, the living and the unborn. "The living are the link between death and life. Those to be born are the buds in the loins of the living and marriage makes it possible for them to germinate and sprout" (Mbiti, 1991).

He who does not get married (by deliberately choosing not to) is destroying the buds which otherwise would sprout and grow on the human tree of life.

Such a man, according to Ndebele custom, was, upon his death, buried with a rat. Among the Pedi, a short burning wooden stick, *serumula*, was pushed into his anus to symbolise the burning of unused buds (Ramose, 1980).

THE TONGA

Introduction
Abridged from *A History of North-Western Zimbabwe since 400 AD*,
by Godfrey Tabona Ncube

The earliest Bantu speakers settled in the Victoria Falls region between 400-500 AD. The use of ceramic style, or tradition, to recognize groups of people suggests that these early farmers were displaced at the end of the ninth century by the Later Iron Age Kalomo group. Around the twelfth century, the Kangila ceramic tradition spread southward from the northern areas of the Batoka plateau into the Victoria Falls region. This tradition lasted until relatively recent times, probably around the end of the eighteenth century. It is from this Kangila group that the Tonga language apparently developed.

The Tonga expanded along the Zambezi valley because the Zambezi River assured them of a perennial water supply. There is evidence to suggest that the areas inhabited by the Tonga in Zimbabwe once extended further south than at present. Northerly migrations and conquest by Shona groups from about the seventeenth century onwards apparently caused some Tonga withdrawals northwards.

Both archaeological and linguistic evidence indicate that the Tonga language is associated with the language of northern Zambia and the Democratic Republic of Congo rather than Zimbabwean languages.

The term 'Tonga' itself has applied to the people of the Middle Zambezi valley and the southern Zambezian plateau since the mid-nineteenth century. Prior to their common identity as Tonga people, it is likely that different names were used to describe the inhabitants of different areas throughout the valley. The term 'Tonga', which was probably a term of foreign origin bestowed by their neighbours, has been interpreted to mean a 'chiefless' people or those who do not recognise a paramount ruler. Although the Tonga on both sides of the Zambezi formed one society, spoke the same language and observed the same customs, there is no evidence of them at any time building a large scale political unit under a paramount ruler. Rather, they were organized into a large number of small scattered independent political units, each with its own ruler.

After colonisation, the Tonga were spared the fate of Land Apportionment because of the general prevalence of tsetse fly in their area of settlement.

Thus they did not lose land to Europeans because Europeans were unwilling to settle in that part of the country and risk contracting human trypanosomiasis. Furthermore, the fact that ox-drawn wagon transportation could not be used over most of the Tonga country discouraged many Europeans from settling there, because they were entirely reliant on ox-wagons for bringing in their supplies.

However, the Tonga were to suffer an even greater uprooting and resettlement, involving more than 23,000 people, in the 1950s. Since the damming of the Zambezi at Kariba would form a lake covering 5180 square kilometres, submerging the Zambezi plain, the lower courses of the tributaries and many of the lower hills, the Federal government embarked on the forced removal and resettlement of all the people below the 488 metre elevation. The movement of the Tonga from the valley was implemented over a 3-year period (1956-58) and the actual transfer of the people from the valley to escarpment was executed in government lorries.

The creation of Lake Kariba provides an example of massive technological development achieved at tremendous economic and social cost to the displaced people. The Valley Tonga lost their valued alluvial river gardens, which had played a major role in staving off famine, and the loss of sacred graves where the lineage spirits had been worshipped and propitiated – this loss was perhaps the most serious and difficult to compensate because its value could not be measured in material terms.

Today the Tonga people are found in Hwange (eastern), Lupane (western/northern), Gokwe North and Nyaminyami/Kariba districts.

Tonga architecture

There are four of us in this human trap, what might be termed a *sikorokoro*. It is a sad euphemism to call it a car. The thing croaks, crackles and judders along. At Dete Cross we turn right towards Tongaland. Wood carvings grace the fringes of the tarred road. Craning giraffes share the shade with bulky hippopotami.

As we continue with our descent into the Zambezi Valley, the scorching heat becomes unbearable. We sweat profusely. The absence of some window panes in the car turns out to be a blessing in disguise.

As we go down I notice some changes in hut architecture. The manner of roofing is different from the tiered fashion that I am used to. However, it is a hut on legs that catches my eye. This is the '*ngazi*', as the Tonga people call it. Today I shall take a closer look at it. But only once we are beyond Siachilaba.

We find Siachilaba a hive of activity. The business centre is well patronized. Several women sit in rows selling dried fish and bundles of fruit that they say improves the taste of porridge. Baobab fruit is also on sale. This queen of trees grows best in hot and dry areas like this.

When our car crackles to a noisy stop, we are invaded by scores of salespeople offering their wares for sale. I disembark to stretch my legs and go into the store. On the verandah men are partaking of a fermented drink. Inside the store the till is ringing continuously. Undoubtedly, there is brisk business here. I buy an issue of *Indonnsakusa-Ilanga* newspaper to entertain myself in the evening.

My companion, who is making her first visit to Tongaland, is curious to see women with their '*nchelwas*' or '*ndombondo*', the Tonga traditional smoking pipes. As we walk back to the car, we see two women holding these pipes. My companion gives the women a long, hard searching look. Back in the car I start the engine and off we go at full throttle.

We get to an *ngazi* very close to the road. I kill the engine instantly. My intention is to take a closer look at the structure, with a view to appreciating its architecture. When I get to Binga, I will ask a few questions relating to it. I do not wish to indulge in speculation and wishful thinking, and recreate a culture and history for the Tonga. The Tonga themselves will tell me all they know about the *ngazi*. My role will be to record their narrations.

At Binga the following day, I meet Diamond Munkuli, Jairos Muzezuru Nyathi, Duncan Sinampande and Cephas Mutale. Jairos has his own sad story of how he became Nyathi. He is actually Munkombwe. When his father went to get a national identity card for him at Lupane, during the troubled days of the Gukurahundi, his father was forced into accepting an Ndebele equivalent of the Tonga Munkombwe. His own children, emphatically, will be called Muzezuru, in recognition of some Zezuru people who looked after him for the first seven years of his life.

Back to the *ngazi*. This is a multi-purpose structure built on a high-platform that rests on stilts. Some have no walls, some have walls plastered on the inside only; while others have their walls plastered on both sides. The *ngazi* for children is usually the one that is plastered on both sides. Their walls are liberally decorated. This is an easy structure to make, it may take just two days to complete one; sometimes it has a verandah, the *dalabanze,* which is unroofed.

This structure, *n'anda yamujulu,* can be used as a sleeping hut, a grain storage hut and a watchtower in the cornfields. The Valley Tonga, before construction of the Kariba Dam in the late 1950s, used to work flood–plain fields and inland fields. They built the *ngazi* in which to sleep while watching over their crops. The whole idea behind elevating the hut was to keep away from the marauding animals, especially the hippopotami.

The Zambezi Valley is a very hot area, and making a wall-less *ngazi*, consisting of a roof and a platform, ensured cooler conditions. Unplastered walls, likewise, improved ventilation.

Cephas Mutale mentions also that herd boys slept in the *ngazi* while the sheep and goats were penned below it. While the boys were expected to keep the predatory animals at bay, the platform of the *ngazi* ensured a dry pen for the livestock.

Only Diamond Munkuli mentions the *ntontomba*. The Tonga men, like virtually all other Bantu men, married several wives. The husband slept in the *ngazi* and his wives would take turns to visit him for conjugal visits.

Duncan Sinampande, with a modern house as his home, has an *ngazi* in which he keeps his grain.

Later, back at the lakeshore lodge where I am staying, as the night wears on, fear engulfs me. There is not a single noise to keep me company. It's so quiet as if a hungry lion is about to bolt from the darkness and pounce on me. This I can't afford - a lion munching away my skull, my brains, my heart, and my soul even. There is no *ngazi* in which to seek shelter. I quickly get into bed and tell myself "it is as safe in this lodge as in a Tonga *ngazi*."

The origin of the name Binga

The following morning, I leave my lodge to experience dawn by the lakeside and join several other creatures in the pomp and pageantry that marks the start of a new day. The distinctive call of the fish eagle announces the advance of the sun. It is a contented and expectant call. The fish that abound in the lake are its breakfast, its lunch and dinner.

Fishermen are prohibited from fishing in this particular area. Super, our attendant, calls it maternity. This is where fish spawn. Just last night I was reading about various dangerous fish. The beautiful tiger fish is said to have teeth that are razor sharp. When removing the hook, use long nosed pliers and keep a very firm grip on the fish in the gill area. Don't throw a tiger fish into the boat, it could bite someone. Even the beautiful ones do bite, eh! I commented to myself quietly.

The next fish is the squeaker. Squeakers come out of the water with a characteristic squeaking noise. They have three very strong barbed fins that can close onto fingers if you grasp its body. This world is no home for the vulnerable and the defenceless. It's the survival of the sharpest.

Then there is the electric cat fish, the most dangerous. This is a mottled, bloated-looking barbed type of fish. It can push out up to 500 volts. Cut your line if you catch one lest it touches your body. There is nothing new in man's discoveries, after all. Nature already has these things. I never imagined a fish could generate up to 500 volts, enough to light up Sankojana Rural Business Centre, Sankonjana School and Sankonjana Rural Health Centre.

I should not end on a sad fishy note. There are less harmful fish that are safe to catch, either for sport or for the pot. This category includes bottlenose, bream, barbel and the ubiquitous matemba.

Other birds join the fish eagle, each with its own song. About an hour from the break of dawn, the chirping from the song-birds is an overwhelming experience. Various insects bring in alto, tenor and unclassified sounds. A lone baboon performs an acrobatic stunt on a mopane tree and caps it with a cacophonous bark that reverberates down the smoke-covered valley. There are many fires burning inland and the smoke settles in the lower valleys.

The rocks on the shore are reflected on the water. The fine breeze creates dancing reflections. An odd fishing rig can be seen returning home with a night's catch of matemba. It's now time for another encounter with Duncan Sinampande.

Today I start with the name Binga. The Tonga word *binga* means to drive or to lead. The man who got the name of Binga used to be under Chief Sikalenge, of the Banenge clan. When it was realised that Chief Sikalenge had too many people under his charge, a man was asked to lead some of these people and start a new chieftainship. The man who led these people was called Binga. The whole district is today named after that man. Sinampande points out that Binga became more famous at the time of colonisation, because he quickly endeared himself to the new white masters. "What does the name Tonga mean?" I ask inquisitively. Sinampande shakes his head and pleads ignorance on the meaning of the name. I tell him what Aeneas Chigwedere suggested as the meaning. It is derived from *'donga wadonga'*, meaning chaos. This suggests that the Tonga people did not have a centralised form of government like the Shona and the Ndebele. Instead, each chief and his people lived independently. Sinampande finds it difficult to disagree with the historian Aeneas Chigwedere. If anything, he confirms his assertion. Unlike in other districts of Matabeleland, there are no headmen in Binga. Sinampande identifies seventeen chiefs. However, he is not sure about Gavula.

He divides these chiefs into the dialects they speak. The Chiwe dialect is spoken by the people of chiefs Siyabuwa, Mola, Sinampande, Sinamusanga, Sinakatenge, Sinamwenda; Siamupa, Sinansegwe and Sinakooma. All these chiefs, with the exception of Siyabuwa, used to live very close to the Zambezi River and were evicted during the construction of the Kariba Dam. The Chiwe dialect is spoken also on the Zambian side. The second dialect of Chinamwenda is spoken by the people under chiefs Sikalenge, Binga, Siansali and Siachilaba. The third dialect, Chinamalundu, is spoken by the people under chiefs Saba and Pashu, and some of the people under Siachilaba.

Chief Sinamagonde, in the Lusulu area, also speaks Chiwe. He and his people were also evicted during the construction of the Kariba Dam. Unlike his fellow Chiwe speakers, he went further inland. Probably he was re-occupying the old Tonga areas such as Nkayi, Lupane and Gokwe that were, at some point, inhabited by the Tonga.

I am interested to know why the Tonga preferred to be near the Zambezi River. Sinampande is quick to come up with an answer. The river is a reliable source of drinking water. Inland areas are dry. Besides, the river provides a consistent supply of fish. The Tonga are fine fishermen who use the harpoon, *ugumba,* with great skill. They also use a fishing basket called *zubo*.

Equally important is the fact that the river flooded its plain during summer months. The Tonga were able to grow crops twice a year on the flood-plain which retained moisture. In summer they grew crops in inland fields. The *ngazi* was built to serve as a watchtower in these inland fields. Thus the forced eviction of the Tonga to make way for the Kariba Dam deprived them of their main source of sustenance.

I bid my good friend farewell and return to my temporary paradise on the shores of Lake Kariba, a real home away from home.

Language corruption: from 'Kasamba bezi' to Zambezi

Through the medium of language, we listen to ourselves. We discover ourselves.

With my moist hand I brush sweat off my forehead. Lethargy overcomes me. Something at the corner of the table catches my eye. A pupil's exercise book. This should bring back fond memories of a nearly forgotten past. Leafing through the tattered book I see a letter. I read it:

"Dear my friend,
Yesterday I am very sick. Come and see me but you can sick I am come and see you but I am sick you not come why I am finish"

I can't laugh at this. A Tonga child is expected, at an early age, to grapple with English, her mother language and Ndebele. Just how much is this child able to communicate with her inner self and bring it to the fore? Flipping through two more pages, I come across another letter, I read it also:

"Dear my friend Thandiwe Mumpande
I want to tell you about your mother My mother is very happer and me is very happer Than we are We are tell other me myself. We prayed to God and then we read English Languege in the Biible. We are finished Munkombwe."

Just yesterday I was flipping through a Gideon's Bible. In all the hotels that I have been to, I have never found a Koran. In the Gideon's Bible there was a rendition of a famous verse, "God so loved the world..." in several languages: English; Portuguese; Spanish; Greek; Chinese; Japanese; Hebrew. No African language other than Swahili. Where is Nguni? Where is Hausa? Can't we be saved through our own languages?

I am face to face with Duncan Sinampande. The office he is operating from is small and unventilated. Through the window I can see Lake Kariba. It is only a few metres away from his office. There is no breeze from this vast body of water.

"What is the name of the river?" I quiz the sweating man. "You mean the lake?" he asks back. "The river that was dammed."

"Kasamba bezi," he says with a big smile. He goes on to explain that this is the river where only those who know (*bezi*) wash (*kusamba*).

Immediately I recall Bleek and his studies of Bantu languages. It's him who coined the word Bantu. How similar these languages are.

Kusamba is Tonga for wash. In Ndebele it is *ukuhlamba*, while the Shona equivalent is *kushamba*.

Kasamba bezi is infested with crocodiles. Foreigners, who don't know the safe spots where to bathe, risk being savaged by the crocodiles. It is interesting to see how the name corrupted into the form of Zambezi.

Pursuing this theme further, Sinampande is quick to point out that several Tonga names and words were corrupted in a similar manner. The Shona/Ndebele interpreters were responsible for this. Look at how the mountain range to the south of the lake has had its name corrupted. On the map it is shown as Chizarira, which is a Shona name. The Tonga name, which was corrupted by a Shona interpreter, is Tujalile, which means to enclose. The range formed a barrier against attacks by Mapunu, the term the Tonga used in reference to the Ndebele.

The Ndebele warriors used to raid the Tonga, who would seek shelter in the mountains or stand their ground with their famed barbed spears. Some of them even crossed the *Kasamba bezi* in boats.

The Tonga language is taught from Grade 1 to Grade 3. Then Ndebele and English are taught in higher grades. The tragedy for the Tonga, though, is that most of the teachers are either Shona or Ndebele, with little or no knowledge of Tonga.

When I consider the importance of language and what it does for a person, I get a sinking feeling. Surely, it must be an inalienable right to communicate in one's own language.

The Tonga nchelwa provides a healthier way of smoking

This is not my first trip to Binga. This trip, however, took on a special appeal. I came with the intention of finding out more about Tonga tradition and I did manage to prise open a few precious shells. Perhaps, this time, I was a bit more fastidious.

Now I have to bid farewell to Super, our attendant. I have to leave behind the energising morning breeze, the sounds of the bush, the tranquillising greens of the vegetation, and the soul-hugging, burning African sunset.

There is just one more interview I wish to carry out before we start on the return journey. Why would a lot of people associate Binga with mbanje/dagga smoking? Who says the Tonga *nchelwa* is used for smoking mbanje? The *nchelwa*, or *ndombondo* or *mfuko* is that artefact that many tourists visiting Binga are keen to catch a glimpse of. It goes by different names, depending on one's dialect. Similarly, the Plateau Tonga call father '*taata*', in another dialect, father is '*ndeende*'.

Cephas Mutale is a ball of energy. He speaks in bombastic tones. Prior to my encounter with Mutale, the humorous Diamond Munkuli had told me about the efforts of a Tonga policeman. He knew his colleagues from other parts of Zimbabwe believed there was mbanje in an *nchelwa*. He wanted to blow this resilient bubble of prejudice. A roadblock was mounted at the Siabuwa turn off. The policeman collected no less than three *nchelwas* from women passengers on the bus. He meticulously dismantled each in the presence of the inquisitive, doubting Thomases. And lo and behold, there was nothing in the *nchelwas* other than *polya*, or tobacco.

Mutale kicks off his defence. The *nchelwa* is used by women. They hold it gracefully against their chests. The long handled gourd contains water through which smoke is inhaled.

Mutale pauses and peers at me as if asking, "Do you hear, you *Mupunu*?" I quickly engineer a facial configuration that reassures him.

"Women don't smoke mbanje. They smoke *polya* and nothing else."

I find myself madly nodding my over-sized skull, which I got courtesy of my father. I am not, for a moment, doubting his story. But there is a question that is going around in my head. What about the menfolk?

Before I throw the question at him, I reflect on the *nchelwa*. Couldn't this be a healthier way of smoking *polya*? Bubbling the smoke through water dissolves some noxious substances. This makes sense, good, healthy sense.

Men don't use an *nchelwa*. Instead, they use *chitete*, a smoking pipe made from a reed. Some call this *mpipi*. Surely, this must be a corruption of the English word pipe. In the Zulu language there is *ipipi*.

Mutale chuckles, as a prelude to his pontification. African men, whether Tonga or not, used to smoke mbanje. And some still do so today. So, why should mbanje smoking be associated with the *nchelwa,* which men don't even use?

I know Ndebele men used to smoke *insangu* in a specially designed apparatus called *igudu. Igudu* was made from a horn. Mbanje smoke was inhaled after it had been bubbled through water. Men used to take turns to inhale the smoke. *'Indaba egudwini'* refers to the talk they indulged in during this smoking extravaganza.

Mutale says the Tonga men enjoyed their mbanje undiluted by bubbling it through water. Grain was placed above the dagga in the pipe. Hot embers were placed on the grain that, in turn, burnt the mbanje. This ensured slower combustion and the result was extended smoking pleasure.

This method, however, did not preclude inhalation of smoke from the burning grain. To obviate this problem, small stone pebbles were placed on top of the mbanje in the pipe. Preferably the hot embers came from a mopane tree. These are hotter and burn much longer than embers from other trees. The pebbles became hot and passed the heat, by conduction, to the mbanje below them. When ignition temperature was reached, the plant leaves started smouldering. The smoke so inhaled was pure mbanje smoke. Unpolluted. Undiluted.

The law that bans mbanje smoking also applies to Binga. If mbanje ravages the health of the Birwa, Kalanga and Venda, it does the same to the Tonga.

Diamond Munkuli and Jairos Nyathi, who have been listening to Mutale's explanation, sit at ease as we prepare to bid each other farewell.

I am a bit nervous. Yesterday our juddering spectacle of a car got stuck in the sandy quagmire just outside Duncan Sinampande's office. Parirenyatwa did, after a long struggle, manage to free our *sikorokoro.*

I pack my pen and paper, take a last look at the glittering waters of Lake Kariba and drag myself out of the office. Through the rear view mirror I see a waving Munkuli and Sinampande. As I approach the T-junction, the human trap steadies a little and I catch a last glimpse of the two men. They are now hardly visible and soon become dying images in the mirror.

Once on the tarmac, I quietly utter the words, "*Ndila kuyanda* Binga" (I love you Binga). I put my right hand out of my paneless window and wave at all the human beings I see around. "Binga *usyale oobotu*". Goodbye, Binga.

Bulumba: Tonga hole-in-the-nose

A TALL, slim, frail old lady puffs benignly at her pipe. Young women mill around selling dried fish, mostly tiger and bream. Despite their polished, tried and tested sales gimmicks, they can't lure me. They only manage to remind me of the Maasai women I met in Kenya.

The lady of the pipe has captured my heart. Wait, I am not given to polygamous tendencies. I take a quick glance at the lady. Yes indeed, there is something below her nose that raises intense curiosity in me. She parts her lips and reveals she has no front teeth on her upper jaw.

I realise there is a language barrier between us preventing conversation. I give her a final parting gaze so as to retain in my mind the image of the well decorated stick stuck through her nose. The lady is said to be a common sight at Siachilaba in Binga district. No sooner do I get to Binga than I look for Duncan Sinampande and Mailos Mugande to enlighten me on what I had seen.

"See, I also have got the hole through my nose", chuckles Sinampande, as he tilts his head to expose the otherwise concealed hole. "It's all part of beautifying oneself," he says, with a broad smile which bares his milky white teeth.

The hole is called *bulumba*. The piece of reed or smooth stick that is pushed through the hole is called *kasita*. My curiosity is excited. I enquire more into the custom. Both sexes used to have their *bulumba* made by specialist women who used sharp thorns from a *moombenge* or *mukoka* tree to make the hole. Once the sharp thorn was pushed through, the sharp end was broken. Healing took place with the thorn in place.

Warm water was used to clean the septic wounds that almost always developed afterwards. As the healing progressed the thorn became loose. A short reed or smooth stick was then inserted into the hole to make it even bigger. With the healing completed, a permanent and longer piece of reed or smooth stick was pushed through. Its two ends were decorated with colourful beads. The reed could be removed if need be, and was usually put on during *ngoma,* a kind of Tonga orchestral ensemble where horns are blown and drums beaten.

Mailos Mugande, being younger than Sinampande, does not have a hole through his nose. The practice fell into disuse, particularly during the 1950s when the Tonga were moved from the Zambezi River ahead of the construction of the Kariba Dam.

Down in the Zambezi Valley there were no schools. Schools were only built when the Tonga moved further inland. For example, in 1959, Manjolo, Sinampande and Samende schools were built by the Methodists. Siabuwa School, upland, was in existence much earlier. The Methodists established a school there in 1948.

Moving upland also brought the Tonga into contact with the people of other ethnic groups who worked on the roads and in the offices. The move to the interior destroyed many Tonga customary practices.

Next I look at Sinampande's ears. Each ear lobe has a hole that was made when Sinampande was very young. Generally, says Sinampande, ear lobe piercing was carried out at a more tender age than the piercing of the nose. For earrings, some Tonga men and women used pieces of soft copper wire. Usually the wires were decorated by coiling silver wire around them. With each ear festooned with lots of these metallic devices, one's beauty was considerably enhanced.

Sinampande goes on to show me marks on his body that he says were also part of beautification. In the area just above his eyebrows is a crescent moon made by incisions. On each cheek there is what he calls a star - consisting of four equally spaced incisions that nearly meet at the centre.

Mr Mugande is pleasantly surprised to see the celestial incisions. Yes, he was aware of Mr Sinampande's hole in the nose, but had never seen his moon and stars. I have also met Sinampande on several occasions, but never noticed these heavenly bodies lightly etched on his dark face.

Incision making is taken to a higher plane among the women. Intricate designs are to be found on their chests and extend to the abdomen. More are to be found on the upper arms. You get an impression of several stars concentrated into patterned lines - the earthly version of the galaxy.

Sinampande promises to tell me at a later date about the woman's four front teeth that were knocked out of her upper jaw. I feel as if a thousand cockroaches are engaged in pre-mating manoeuvres in my stomach. I bid the two colleagues goodbye.

Zambezi River intricately tied to Tonga culture

Although Africans were an illiterate people, they had various ways and means of preserving their history, culture, ideas on governance, interpersonal relationships and philosophy, among other things. Proverbs, riddles, songs, lullabies, praise poetry and folk-tales are important repositories of a people's wisdom.

I chose the proverbs and wise sayings as my first port of call. Tragically, among most African peoples, the process of creating new proverbs was arrested at the point of colonisation. Most proverbs currently in use predate the colonial era. A close look at existing historical proverbs illustrates relations between nature, the cosmos and the inanimate world and mankind. On another plane, proverbs record human relations and behaviour expected among persons of a given society.

When Western culture was introduced, the new social relations, values and items of material culture did not find their way into new proverbs. The old and sometimes irrelevant proverbs continued to hold sway. The same applied to folk-tales whose character belonged to an historical past. Unfortunately, constant recourse to the unknown past has resulted in current generations of learners often being uninterested in folk-tales and proverbs.

Interestingly, songs did not meet with a similar fate. Colonial and post independence themes, issues, characters and cultural artefacts have found their way into current songs - hence their popularity.

Among the Tonga, therefore, one would expect proverbs to relate to the Zambezi. As indicated earlier, the name Zambezi is a corruption of *Kasamba bezi*, meaning where those well versed with the river can bathe. The big river, *mulonga mupati,* is infested with crocodiles. Knowledge about the river is indispensable to those who wish to fish, board canoes, bathe or cross the river. Within the river are to be found shallow areas, *chito* (plural, *zito*) which one can take advantage of to ford the river. The Tonga, found on both sides of the river, viewed the river, not as a barrier, but as a communication link. Canoes, *bwato,* were used to cross the river. Boatmen used oars, *nsoke,* for propelling the boats.

The words *bwato* and *chito* have found their way into Tonga proverbs, as illustrated by Isaac Mumpande who has painstakingly collected these for eventual publication. '*Bwato tabulindi muntu, bulindilwa aachito*' literally means the owner of the canoe does not wait for intending travellers, instead, travellers should wait for him at the crossing point.

As is the case with all other African proverbs, Tonga proverbs have a primary or literal meaning and a secondary or figurative meaning. Quite often, the first meaning is lost and the second survives. The world of the proverb changes, but the meaning survives. For example, the saying '*selidumela emansumpeni*' may have lost primary meaning to the present generation. However, its secondary meaning, 'success is near', is still known. One would have to know about *ithunga* (milk pail) and that it had lugs, *insumpa*, near the top of the pail, for holding it with one's knees, in order to appreciate its first meaning. When the milk pail is nearly full, at the level of the lugs, the sound changes and success is near.

'*Sibwato banda muntu*' is another Tonga proverb, which hinges on the use of the Zambezi River for transportation across or along it. *Sibatwo* means owner of the canoe and *banda* means to call out loudly. The boatman was expected to call out the names of his passengers as he approached the *chito*. Passengers should get to the *chito* before the boatman arrives.

The boat was carved from a big tree trunk and there is a proverb that gives advice to the carpenter. *Sibwato kubezela munzila bakulaye beenda.* This is advice to the carpenter/boat owner (*sibwato*) to carve *(kubeza)* his boat *(bwato)* near a footpath *(munzila)* so that travellers *(beenda)* offer him advice. This compares with the Ndebele proverb that says '*injobo enhle ithungelwa ebandla*'. The primary meaning is to sew a blanket of beautiful colours in public, while the second is advice for one to seek assistance and guidance from those with the requisite knowledge. It's a caution to 'Mr Know-it-all'.

At the same time the Zambezi was perceived as a treacherous river that could sweep away anyone trying to cross it. What made it even more treacherous was the fact that on the surface its waters looked still. But the lower waters ran swiftly. *Kalonga* (river) *kayibembe* (still/quiet) *nkikatola* (sweeps you away). This is sound advice against being deceived by outside/superficial appearances.

In view of the treachery of the river, travellers were strongly warned against attempting to cross the river on their own. *Simwenda alike kakamutola kalonga.* A lone traveller is swept away by the river - and there is no one to report the tragedy.

The Zambezi River holds a large volume of water; however, all the water it holds is fed into it by smaller tributaries. '*Mulonga uzula abuyoboyobo*', in Tonga. '*Umfula uqcwaliswa yizifudlana*', the Ndebele would say. Small things add up to something big. A million dollars consist of cents. One should not reject a gift however small it might be. Such gifts, put together, add up to something big.

The name of the river *Kasamba bezi* suggests that those who know it well may take a bath in it - provided they know where *zito* (shallow places) occur. Where the water is shallow, one can quickly see an advancing crocodile, *ntale*. *Chito nchuzibide chilumya ntale*. *Nchuzibide* means the one (shallow place) you are familiar with, and *chilumya* means being bitten. Even when you travel or stand on a shallow place, be careful, you could still be bitten by a crocodile.

When a people encounter a new environment, they coin new proverbs based on their observations. Whereas in the past the Ndebele used to say, '*ukuwanda kwaliwangabathakathi*' today they say, '*ukwanda kwaliwa yifamili planingi*'. The original, witches are not happy to see people multiplying has been modernized to, the family planning people do not want to see people multiplying as a result of birth control methods they are teaching the people.

A close scrutiny of the current and historical proverbs lays bare a people's experiences. It also holds the hope of discovering historical relationships among the various people of Africa. A lot more than the land was lost during colonisation.

The Dombe language has no written form

A hard knock shatters the peace of my office in the Mhlahlandlela Government Complex in Bulawayo. "Come in!"
A short bespectacled man, bubbling with confidence, rushes in. He is George Ndlovu. He has come to relate the story of his people, the Dombe. My articles on the Tonga people nudged him into action. Hurriedly, George Ndlovu lowers his body into a chair. After the business-like ritual of greetings, he rummages in his black bag. My inquisitive and prying eyes follow his movements. A short while later, he proffers a Catholic catechism manual. It's written in the Nambiya language.
There is clearly some sense of urgency about the man. Anxiety and impatience are now indelibly etched on his tense face. It turns out that the Dombe language has no written form. In the Hwange District, where the Dombe people live, Nambiya predominates. The Dombe were already in the Hwange district when the Nambiya, called the Makaranga by the Dombe, arrived. A dying language. A dying culture. Reasons enough for deep concern.
George Ndlovu relates his story. The Dombe, or more appropriately the Leya, are a Tonga people. They speak a dialect of Tonga. They came from across the Zambezi River to settle in what is now the Hwange District. George Ndlovu identifies in particular the three clans of Mapeta, Chenya and Ngonzi. This was a long time before the arrival of the Nambiya.
The Leya who remained behind in Zambia called those venturing across the Zambezi River Balombe, which means, brave young men. The area they were venturing into was densely forested. The Leya are one of several Tonga sub-groups, which include the Toka, the Ila, the Bawe and the ruling Mwemba who straggled the Zambezi River.
According to oral sources, Ndlovu says, the Mwemba were conquered by the Kololo of Sebetuane, the Sotho chief whose people were defeated at Dithakong by a Griqua-Korana force put together by Dr Robert Moffat (uMtshede) of Kuruman. Sebetuane proceeded to conquer more Tonga peoples and the Lozi of Lewaanika.
Other than Chief Dingani, whose totem is Baambala or Mpala in Ndebele, there are no Dombe chiefs in the Hwange district. Chief Dingani is thought to descend from Chief Sekute, whose people lived above the Victoria Falls. The other chiefs, namely Hwange (or Zanke in Ndebele), Shana and Nekatambe, are Nambiya. Chief Mvuthu Mlotshwa is Ndebele. He is the

descendant of the famous Xukutshwayo of Entembeni.

Dombe culture has, to a very large extent, been submerged by Nambiya and Ndebele cultures. The surnames of Munsaka, Mwemba and Muleya have become Ndlovu, Nyoni and Tshuma, respectively. As is the case among the Tonga, Dombe children should get their surnames from their father's mother. Being a Tonga people, the Dombe used to be matrilineal. Current practice is for the children to get their surnames from their father. The patriarchal and patrilineal Ndebele and Shona are influencing their culture.

The Dombe, like other African people, are great lovers of music and dance. The *musimbo,* or *mumbambalikwa,* is the huge four legged drum, approximately 1,3 metres high, played during ceremonies such as *malilwe* or *chipelu,* the bringing home ceremony, and the *miliya* rain making ceremony. The *nkonkolo* is a smaller drum that accompanies the *musimbo.* Sticks are used to beat the drum. Music from the Dombe drums is playing in George Ndlovu's mind. His uplifted hand is clutching the air. He is imitating one who is playing the *nsaka,* a hand rattle. For leg rattles, the Dombe use *masangusangu* (gourds).

The *vulumu* or *namalwa* drum is probably unique to the Dombe. George Ndlovu calls it a friction drum. It has a hide fixed around one end of the drum and a reed is attached to the hide's centre. By rubbing a hand against the moist reed, a frictional sound is produced. This musical instrument is essentially extinct. George concludes his story by explaining some Dombe names. *Ndangababi* means to look for the bad or ugly. *Lambo* is derived from *Sinelambo,* a Dombe tribesman who lived in that area. *Kulisina* is to commit suicide by hanging.

THE SHONA

This section is based on an interview with James Dzvova on 1 December, 2000 at Johannesburg International Airport.

The Shona, who comprise the largest ethnic group in Zimbabwe, arrived on the Zimbabwean scene more than 1000 years ago. They included the Nambiya and the Kalanga. Some Shona are found in western Mozambique and southern Zambia where they are known as the Lozi. Today the Shona fall into a number of sub-ethnic groups: the Karanga, Zezuru, Manyika, Kore-Kore and Ndau.

Their earliest known ancestor is Tovera (Thobela), whose son was Mambiri (Mambili). Mambiri's son was the famous Murenga Sororenzou. Murenga is the Shona ancestor who operates from the Njelele Mwali shrine. His son was Chaminuka and his daughter Nehanda. Oral tradition claims that the Shona came from Tanzania, where both Tovera and Mambiri lived. The journey to the south is associated with Murenga and Chaminuka. The latter crossed the Zambezi River and entered the territory that is known today as Zimbabwe.

One of Chaminuka's better known sons was Kutamadzoka, alias Mutiusinazita or Mabwemashava. It was he who became the first Mutapa. He lived in the present day Waddilove area. Kutamadzoka's brother, Chigwangu, proceeded south and built Great Zimbabwe near Masvingo. For this building, Chigwangu became known as Rusvingo, meaning stone wall. Construction started in about 1100 AD.

In the area where he built, Rusvingo found the Dziva-Hungwe people, that is the people of the Dziva, Hungwe and Hove totems. It is thought that these earlier inhabitants were used as labourers during the construction of Great Zimbabwe. Rusvingo became the Mutapa after the death of his brother Kutamadzoka.

By 1500 the Zimbabwe State was no more. The demise of the Zimbabwe State led to the establishment of a number of provinces. Guruuswa, located to the west, was created by Mukwati and Torwa. Shangwe (meaning drought) was established in the north of the country by Mafunga who went there in search of salt. The province of Manyika was founded by Chikanga in about 1460. The province of Manyika came about as an offshoot of Barwe (meaning maize), which was founded by Makombe, a son of Kauswere, a brother of Kutamadzoka. The province of Kore-Kore was established by Mutota and Chingoo.

Another province was that of Uteve, whose chief was Sachiteve. In about 1700, Chikosha, whose two sons were Rukweza and Zimutsvi, left Uteve. He headed eastwards, but died during the trek. His sons settled in Bikita where they founded the Duma confederacy. Like Mutota, Chikosha was a descendant of Dlembeu.

Dlembeu's father, Chibatamtosi, was a Soko. Dlembeu was thus initially a Soko, but later because the first Moyo, hence Mutota was Moyo and the chiefs in the Duma country are still Moyo Chirandu. Some of the chiefs in Duma country are: Chiwara, Mutindi, Mukanganwi, Pfupajena, Makore, Mazungunye, Murinye, Mugabe, Mukaro, Nhema (in Zaka).

Anther province that was established was that of Mbire based around Hwedza.

The Shona are renowned for their stone architecture. Stone walled structures are found in several parts of Zimbabwe, northern South Africa and northern and north-eastern Botswana.

Archaeological research shows that the first stone buildings were constructed at Mapungubwe near the confluence of the Limpopo and Shashi rivers. These ruins are associated with the State of Mapungubwe, which was succeeded by the Zimbabwe State.

When the Zimbabwe State fell, the Torwa State (in Guruuswa or western Zimbabwe), based at Khami, came into being. The Mutapa State in the north near the Zambezi River also came into being.

Link between Mapungubwe and the Shona

ON March 6, 2000, the South African Broadcasting Corporation's Channel 1 broadcast a documentary entitled 'Mapungubwe, Secrets of the Sacred Hill'. Mapungubwe, a flat topped hill, is located on the South African side of the Limpopo River, near its confluence with the Shashi River. It was the site of Southern Africa's first organised state system. It is here that the Zimbabwe tradition started, characterised by stone architecture and burnished clay pots. Initially, according to the SABC programme, settlement was based at Schroda and, later, at K2. The former was located north east of Mapungubwe. Its growth and pre-eminence was attributable to strong trade links with the east coast where Islamic traders provided beads, ceramics and cloth in exchange for ivory, hides, ostrich feathers and later gold.

In about 1000 AD, the centre of activity shifted from Schroda to K2. At this time, a powerful royal elite emerged and took control of the lucrative trade in beads. In fact, they were making their own beads in competition to those supplied by the Swahili traders from the east coast.

While at Schroda, cattle played a pivotal role in the economy – giving rise to socio-economic differentiation – their role diminished at K2. Trade markets then took centre stage, increasing social stratification. The gulf in wealth between royals and commoners widened. The former sought a new site where settlement would reflect the prevailing socio-economic differentiation. Off to the hill of Mapungubwe they went.

The ruling elite occupied the highest point on the hill with the middle level royals occupying the next highest levels. The commoners occupied the lowest levels in the valleys down below. In addition, dry stone walling was begun, more as an expression of power, wealth and prestige than defence. This physical expression of status came to characterise later stone settlement at Great Zimbabwe, Khami, Danangombe, Bumbusi and other Zimbabwe tradition sites.

The situation at Old Bulawayo is comparable. The Royal Enclosure, *Isigodlo,* where King Lobengula Khumalo and his queens lived, occupied the highest point on the low hill. The peripheral settlement, where the commoners lived, occupied the lower ground.

The identity of the people who occupied Mapungubwe has never been in doubt. It was the ancestors of the Shona/Kalanga. In Kalanga, as in Sotho, Mapungubwe means the place of the jackal. In Venda, it means the place of the rock, according to the SABC broadcast.

Professor Tom Huffman has used this evidence to suggest that the Shona came into Zimbabwe from the south. It is difficult to completely reject his theory. The subsequent spread of *madzimbabwe* seems to coincide with the movement of the Shona/Kalanga.

Mapungubwe began to decline and was deserted by the turn of the thirteenth century. A new-site, but of greater grandeur, emerged at Great Zimbabwe. This suggests a movement of the people, specifically the Shona/Kalanga to Great Zimbabwe. Some people moved eastwards into Venda country.

After the decline of Great Zimbabwe, the tradition of stone building was taken to various places. The emergence of stone walled sites does coincide with the arrival of the Shona in those areas. Khami was built by the Torwa who came from Great Zimbabwe. The Mutapa State in the Zambezi valley continued the stone building tradition. More Shona people left for Vendaland and there continued the tradition at Thulamela.

Even during the Rozvi Empire the tradition continued and, where sites were established, this marked the arrival of the Rozvi, who were Shona. Danangombe, Manyanga, Bumbusi and lesser known sites such as those found on Sankonjana-Dume hills, Tokwana across the Thekwane River and Mwalana near Manguba are examples of these (Interview with Saul Gwakuba Ndlovu, 2000).

The scenario painted above strongly supports a southern origin of the Shona/Kalanga. This seems to conflict with oral tradition that suggests that the Shona came from the north. True, they initially came from the north and some may have been left behind along the way. However it does seem there is strong evidence for a south-north movement and spread of the Zimbabwe tradition.

When the royals were established on the Mapungubwe hill, they elected to be buried on the hill. Their lofty status was to be retained beyond the grave. During excavations on Mapungubwe, various items were unearthed in the graves of the royals. If the people who lived on Mapungubwe hill were Shona/Kalanga, one would expect the finds to be related to the traditions of these people. This was the case.

The Kalanga, indeed most African people, believe in life after death. "... death is not a complete destruction of the individual. Life goes on beyond the grave" (Mbiti, 1991).

"It is believed that a human being does not completely die, but he/she goes to another world where he/she meets his/her ancestors," says Saul Gwakuba Ndlovu.

If one were a hunter, it was believed one would continue as a hunter in the next world. Hence from a cultural perspective, the hunter was buried together with his weapons - these were placed beside him in the grave. Such weapons were the bow and arrow (*nsebe ne dadi*), spear (*thumo*) or a harpoon (*ngobe*).

However, if the person was a herbalist, or spirit medium, he was not buried with his regalia, as these were items for inheritance. Items in this category included the headgear of a woman with the spirit of a lion *(humba)*.

It was believed also that when a man or woman died, his/her spirit would need to be guided to the next world by the animal that was his/her totem. In this regard, the animal representing the totem was moulded with clay and fired. The totemic model and spiritual guide to the next world was placed next to the corpse. So, models of animals such as elephant, zebra, lion, impala and hippopotamus were interred with the corpse - depending on one's totem.

In the case of a man or woman survived by his/her children, a number of pieces of dry stalks of maize or sorghum were thrown into the grave. The number of pieces corresponded with the number of surviving children. This was followed by the utterance of the following words, "There are your children. You have gone with them all. Do not come back and bother them" (Interview with Saul Gwakuba Ndlovu, 2000).

Among the Kalanga three animals are never used as totems. The first is the honey badger (*selele* or *umantswane*). This animal is believed to be tough and stubborn, traits that are not cherished. Interestingly, the Ndebele use its skin to treat a new-born baby's fontanelle (*ukwethesa inkanda).*

The second animal is the antbear (*whombela/isambane)* that is associated with wizards and witches. In several African societies the animal is regarded as transport for the wizards and witches on their nocturnal errands.

The third animal is the rhinoceros (*chipembere/ubhejane*). A gold model of a rhino was unearthed from a royal grave on the top of Mapungubwe hill. Among the Kalanga the rhino is regarded as a royal animal and no one is allowed to use it as their totem. The rhino symbolises power, strength, resilience and aggression. The belief among the Shona is that when a rhinoceros has eaten cactus (*mukonde)* it becomes even more aggressive and goes wild with rage (Interview with Mr F. T. Manyuruke, 2000).

Likening kings to wild and powerful creatures was common to several groups in Africa. Some of the kings were likened to elephants (*indlovu),* eagles (*ingqungqulu),* lions *(isilwane)* or snakes (*indlondlo).*

The king was thus buried with a model rhinoceros to symbolise his power, strength and status. To drive the point further home, the rhinoceros was not made from clay but from pure gold. The choice of gold symbolised royal wealth.

The rhino was so highly regarded that hunters were expected to present it to the king if they happened to kill one. However, if distance or some physical barrier did not allow this, hunters were expected to present to the king the dead rhino's horn, heart, liver, bile and testes (Interview with Saul Gwakuba Ndlovu).

The magnificent Great Zimbabwe

One of the exhibitors at the Zimbabwe International Book Fair in Harare was my former history teacher at Mazowe Secondary School, Ken Mufuka, now a professor in the United States. He and I had the experience of launching our books together – *Madoda Lolani Incukuthu*, for me, and *Matters Of Conscience* for him.

I am nestled in one corner of the stand to gather as much information as I can on Zimbabwe's premier monument, Great Zimbabwe. In all of Africa south of the Sahara, no historical monument challenges Great Zimbabwe in grandeur and architectural splendour.

Early whites who visited the monument had problems acknowledging black people as having been responsible for the design and building of such a magnificent construction. They attributed the building of Great Zimbabwe to the Phoenicians.

"Great Zimbabwe was built by the Bantu referred to in Portuguese historical records as the Kalanga. The Zimbabwe State, headquarters at Great Zimbabwe, flourished from 1100 AD to 1500 AD," says Professor Mufuka.

It is generally agreed that the earliest dry stone walling, such as that found at Great Zimbabwe, was carried out at Mapungubwe. When Mapungubwe declined as a trade and political centre, Great Zimbabwe, situated to the north-east across the Limpopo River, was built.

Great Zimbabwe was built of granite, found in great abundance in the area. A wall made of stone is called *rusvingo* (plural *masvingo*). In Nambiya the word is *luswingo* (plural *masvingo*).

"Construction of the capital of the Zimbabwe State was done off season, just like the Egyptian pyramids. No slave labour was used," says Professor Mufuka emphatically.

Tributary chiefs sent their subjects to undertake construction work. Granite blocks were obtained by applying fire to the stone and then pouring cold water onto the hot rock. Sudden cooling and contraction caused the rock to split. Rocks so obtained were chiselled into the required rectangular blocks. Rock extraction is done in the early morning when the temperatures are low, or in winter. Certain members of the Mugabe family still carry out the art of rock extraction and chiselling.

Essentially, there are two major structural components at Great Zimbabwe, the hill top structures and the acropolis in the valley down below. The imposing structures in the valley were the abode of the senior wife (*vahosi)*, so thinks the professor. The solid conical tower within the enclosure symbolised a granary, *dura*. Its existence would most likely have symbolised wealth. Imposing walls did not have a defensive role, rather, they gave a visual impression of power and wealth. They stood as testimony to the socio-economic differences of the people that lived in the sprawling city. Professor Mufuka thinks the entrances to the enclosure were not guarded – suggesting low key security associated with the senior wife. One such queen mentioned in oral sources is Mateya.

Real power at Great Zimbabwe seems to have been concentrated at the hill top, where the king and the chief priest lived. The powerful live at the top. The approach to the building was difficult and the entrances were narrow and guarded. This is in line with its being the abode of the most powerful persons in the state. Chidyamatamba is mentioned in legends as having been a king at one time during the heyday of the Zimbabwe State.

The hilltop was the seat of political and religious power. The king symbolised the former, while the chief priests epitomised the latter. This dual separation of powers was characteristic of Shona society. It provided checks and balances on the king to ensure he did not commit excesses.

So Great Zimbabwe was not only a political centre, it was also an important religious citadel. Early whites who visited the ruins found the Mugabes, who still considered the place a religious centre. Missionaries at Morgenster Mission also recorded the religious significance of the place. A clay pot (*pfuko*) with legs found at Great Zimbabwe also has religious meaning. The pot, like the soapstone bowls, was used in divination, *kushopera*.

There is a tradition that says that fire ceremonies took place at Great Zimbabwe. Runners from the outlying areas came to Great Zimbabwe at the start of each new year to obtain a fresh burning log. This custom compares with that of the Ndebele. At the start of the new season when crops ripened, medicines for *ukuchinsa* (partaking of the first fruits) were obtained from the capital town (*koMkhulu*), where *ukuchinsa* was performed before all other areas did so.

The fire ceremony was carried out so as to maintain political and religious supremacy and hegemony over the people of the state. Annually, that hegemony was renewed, with subjects reaffirming their allegiance.

"Great Zimbabwe controlled trade with the east. If you look at the aerial map of the area, you will see a valley that leads to the Save River and thence to the Mozambique coast where there was a trading post," says Professor Mufuka.

Gold was the chief trading commodity in exchange for beads and cloth. A similar scenario happened at Mapungubwe a few centuries earlier. After five centuries Great Zimbabwe was abandoned, the stone building tradition spreading to other areas.

The origins of Khami Ruins

The Khami Ruins, like the Great Zimbabwe Ruins, belong to the Zimbabwe tradition whose main characteristic was building in stone. Stone architecture was a feature of Zimbabwe, South Africa (the north-west), Botswana (the north-east) and Mozambique between the eleventh and eighteenth centuries.

The decline of Great Zimbabwe around 1450 AD could have been the result of general environmental decline or loss of control of the trade routes to the East coast or simply succession crises.

The Shona at Great Zimbabwe practised collateral chieftainship succession, just as they do today, with the chieftainship moving from brother to younger brother. When it was Mutota's turn to succeed to the throne, his candidature was contested. It was alleged he was born out of an incestuous relationship (Chigwedere, 1980). As a result he and Chingoo moved north to found the Mutapa State in the Dande area.

Meanwhile, Torwa, who was also involved in the succession wrangle, struck due west and established a new state based at Khami.

Torwa introduced the stone building tradition to the south-western part of Zimbabwe. Prior to the arrival of Torwa and his people, the area he moved into, which extended into Botswana and the north-western Transvaal, was occupied by the Kalanga of the Leopard's Kopje culture, which existed from the end of the first millennium to about the fifteenth century (Rasmussen and Rubert, 1990).

The movement of people from Great Zimbabwe resulted in more areas of Zimbabwe engaging in stone architecture. A similar phenomenon took place during the times of the Changamire/Rozvi State when Sawanga led the Nambiya north and introduced the stone building tradition to the north-western parts of Zimbabwe. His first stone capital was based at Shangano while the second was sited at Bumbusi near Sinamatella.

It seems that the word Khami is a corrupted version. Two possible explanations have been proffered. One is that the name Khami derived from the Kalanga word *kama*, meaning to milk. *Nkami* would therefore probably refer to the milkman who looked after King Tjibundule's cattle in the area where the Plumtree road crosses the Khami River.

Oral sources recognise the territorial claims of the Ngwato of Botswana over an area extending north to the Khami River (interviews with Paul R. Dube, 1999 and Fiti Nare, 1985). The other possible explanation is therefore that both the river and the ruins are named after the Ngwato King, Kgama. His people retreated from the Khami area towards Ndolwane, where there is also a place called Kame, and then further south to Mengwe, Tutume and Serowe. Indeed two areas, namely Raditladi and Mpoengs, in western Zimbabwe are named after two of the Ngwato king's sons.

Khami was the seat of both economic and political power in the south-west from around 1450 to 1700 AD, when the Rozvi established the Changamire State in the same area.

Khami, the second largest stone-built complex, displayed certain characteristics that set it apart from Great Zimbabwe. The latter's walls, with rounded entrances, were free standing and concealed huts within them. At Khami, however, there were tiered platforms created by the stone walls that held back the soil. Huts were built on the top of these platforms - making them visible to someone down below.

"The platforms were connected by a system of passages, covered entrances and *dhaka* walls. Thus, while the elite people at Great Zimbabwe and related sites secluded themselves within stone wall enclosures, the Khami elite exposed themselves, another way of symbolically expressing status"(Pwiti, 1997).

Pottery retrieved at the Khami site includes elaborate long–necked jars. Several amateur and professional archaeologists undertook excavation work at the Khami site, including R.N. Hall (between 1900 and 1910), David Randall – MacIver (1905) and K.R. Robinson (1947).

Decorations at Khami are more elaborate than those at Great Zimbabwe. Patterns include chevron, herringbone, chequered and dentelle designs.

The ruins, located some 21 kilometres west of Bulawayo, are spread over a large area, 40 hectares of which were declared a national monument in 1938. The main structures of the complex are the Hill ruins (on top of a hill surrounded by tiered retaining walls), the Cross ruins (with a Maltese cross whose builder is unknown) and the Precipe ruin (now partially submerged by the waters of the Khami Dam).

Living within the Hill Complex was the king, his wives and associates, while the commoners lived down in the valley area. Spatial organisation at Khami again reflected the socio-economic status of the residents.

Residents of Khami, revered and known as *Izintaba zika Mdladla* (Khami Mountain) by the Ndebele, took part in external trade. They imported glass beads, glass and ceramics and exported gold and ivory. Unfortunately, the ruins were ransacked for gold ornaments by the Rhodesian Ancient Ruins

Company Ltd. after colonial occupation.

The Torwa State was conquered by the Rozvi from the central part of Zimbabwe. Their rulers, who used the title of Mambo, built a new capital at Danangombe (Dlodlo ruins), with several satellites such as Naletale, Zinnjanjaja (Regina) and Intaba Zika Mambo.

The stone building tradition continued under the Mambos as indicated by Mambo Nitjasike's praises:

Mulu yobupfuko
Isingabakigwe
Ngelupango
Gunopfusiwa ngolukonye
Inobakigwa ngemabwe.

'The calf that head butts the fence
That is not enclosed by means of wooden poles
Which get destroyed by worms
It is enclosed by stones.' (Saul Gwakuba Ndlovu)

Legend of a four-eyed boy

DIFFERENT societies have different perceptions of disabled people. In the Bikita district of Masvingo, there is a well-known myth surrounding a disabled person called Nyameso.

Bikita district is dominated by the Duma people of the Moyo totem. Their *chidao* is Gono Chirandu. The Duma left the Zambezi Valley to settle in the Great Zimbabwe area before moving out to Uteve in western Mozambique. In about 1700 they left Uteve to settle in the area between the Save River and Great Zimbabwe. Most elders in the area are aware that they came from the east, where they had become closely associated with the Ndau such as the Sitholes. As a Moyo people, the Duma have a common ancestry with the Rozvi Moyo.

Many Shangani/Ndau people left their area to settle among the VaDuma. While working on the biography of former ZIPRA commander Alfred Nikita Mangena, I discovered that the Mangenas (Manyurapasi) are an example of a people under Sotshangane who moved into the Duma area and became Shona. They trekked further west as far as Mberengwa. Some of the Ndau continued to move in a westerly direction until they entered Matabeleland. They had become Moyo through association with the Dumas – whose chief's daughter was given in marriage to a Mangena man. They became Moyo by co-option, to use Aeneas Chigwedere's terminology.

When the Duma settled in the Bikita district they fought the Shiri and the Tembo people. Stories are told of one Pfupajena, a brave warrior, who declared that the Duma empire had no boundaries. The man was so brave he came to overshadow chiefs such as Mukanganwi and Mazungunye.

Another people who came to settle in Bikita were the Rozvi who had been displaced from Matabeleland by the Ndebele. The people of Jiri (to which house the Mambo Tjilisamulu belonged), Mutinhima and Gumunyu sought refuge among the VaDuma. However, Mbavhu's descendants went to Hwedza where Chief Svosve gave them refuge (Chigwedere, 1980).

Among the people who went to Hwedza are descendants of Tumbare. Some of them later left Hwedza and drifted in a south-westerly direction towards Buhera, Gutu and Bikita. They are still found in the three districts, although a few interviewed recently only trace their origins to Hwedza.

In the 1960s some of the Rozvi who had settled in Bikita were moved out to Gokwe where the Jiri chieftainship still exists. One or two Tumbares (Bhebhe or Bepe) went with this group to settle in Gokwe.

Within the districts of Bikita all the chiefs belong to the Duma ethnic group. The chiefs are Mukanganwi, Mazungunye, Budzi, Ziki and Mabika.

Some more Duma chiefs are found in adjoining districts such as Zaka (Chief Bota and Nhema), Gutu (Chiefs Makore, Chiwara and Chikwanda) and Masvingo (Chiefs Mugabe {who has become Shumba}, Murinye and Shumba).

The story goes that a four-eyed boy called Nyameso was born in Chief Mazungunye's area. The child's parents reported the unusual occurrence to the chief, who thought that there was a curse on his people. The Chief ordered the child to be killed.

"Apparently Chief Mazungunye's cousin, Chief Mukanganwi, was against the child being killed," says Lawrence Jenjezwa, who hails from Bikita.

On hearing that her child was to be killed, the mother of Nyameso ran away with her baby. One legend says the mother went and lived in the rugged mountain caves on Mount Rumedzo. According to this version of the legend the mother got water from a perennial well at the foot of the mountain. The well is called *tsime raNyameso* - the well of the four-eyed boy, Nyameso. While searching for food, the mother saw a green insect and started feeding her child with it. The insect is what is known as the *harurwa* or *harugwa*, which is now regarded as a delicacy.

When Nyameso was older and was told about Chief Mazungunye's plan to kill him, he decided to go back and face him. When he arrived back in the village some people ran away, but eventually he was accepted into the community. His father then sent word to Chiefs Mukanganwi and Mazungunye to come to see him.

"However, when Chief Mazungunye came face to face with Nyameso, he collapsed and died," says Lawrence Jenjezwa.

N'angas were consulted and the late chief was found guilty of having attempted to commit a heinous crime by trying to kill an innocent, defenceless child just because he was disabled.

Chief Mukanganwi decided that the four-eyed boy be given a portion of land, *dunhu,* over which to rule. Nyameso thus became a *sadunhu* (headman) under Chief Mukanganwi. This is how the headmanship of Nerumedzo came into being - a lasting reminder of how Chief Mazungunye nearly committed a crime by ordering the death of the disabled child.

Following the death of Chief Mazungunye, it was agreed among the Duma families under Chief Mukanganwi and Chief Mazungunye that anyone ordained as Chief Mazungunye could never set foot on Headman

Nerumedzo's soil. This is so up to today (interviews with Lawrence Jenjezwa, Esther Kanjaga and Pheneas Masendeke).

Furthermore, anyone who became Chief Mazungunye would not meet face to face with any Headman Nerumedzo. This is the case to this day.

"So, if Chief Mazungunye wants to do anything in that part of his chiefdom under Headman Nerumedzo, he has to send a representative to do it on his behalf," says Lawrence Jenjezwa.

Nyameso, Headman Nerumedzo, later married and had several sons. His people, though Duma of Moyo Chirandu, came to be called vaRumedzo, which distinguishes them from the rest of the Dumas. Nyameso's *harurwa* were made into a special dish for his children and a revered area, *jiri*, was set aside for the *harurwa*.

The vaRumedzos' connection with the *harurwa* has earned them praise salutations that the rest of the Duma don't enjoy. They go like this:

Maita Fuve (Thank you *fuve* (a sour *harurwa*))

Chimwazando (drinker of dew/sap)

VariMambiru (those staying in Mambiru's shrine)

Apparently, Mambiru is the place where Nyameso was buried.

The *harurwa*, green insects the size of a big cockroach, appear suddenly on a sunny day in April or May, around the time rapoko flowers. There is no pre-warning of their arrival. A whining sound of millions of airborne insects marks their arrival.

The creatures appear around 10am and hover in the sky until about 4pm when they begin to settle on a *jiri*. A *jiri* is a thicket of dense vegetation that includes, among other trees, *msasa*, *motondo* and *mishuku*.

Year after year the insects settle in the same specially reserved *jiri* where taboos preserve the thicket. When the vaRumedzo hear the sound of the *harurwa*, they send scouts to check the *jiri* to see if the *harurwa* are there.

Origins of the VaRemba

Kufakunesu Hamandishe retrieves a booklet from his desk drawer. It is a prayer book entitled *Salah*. I suspect this is Arabic. Just what is the connection between Hamandishe from Gutu and Arabic writing?

Hamandishe belongs to a group of people known as VaRemba or VaMwenyi (AbaLemba in Ndebele). They claim descent from an Arab man.

"The Lemba have existed as small groups all the way from the Nyanga plateau to the Soutpansberg ..." (Beach, 1997).

However, Beach discards as speculation any suggested link with the Arabs "... a great deal of speculative writing has been published by unscientific writers who claim to see them (the VaRemba) as descendants of the early Muslim Arabs, pre-Muslim Arabs or even Jews."

That there were Arabs on the East Coast is not in doubt. Both the Mapungubwe and Zimbabwe States traded with them. In fact, the capitals of the two states owed their growth largely to the lucrative trade with the East Coast.

Posselt penned the following words with regard to the origins of the VaRemba. "Judging by the features of some natives, there certainly has been an admixture of Semitic blood due to their intercourse with the early Arab traders who had settled on the East Coast and penetrated far inland."

According to the traditions of the VaRemba, their origin dates back to the days of Munhumutapa. "An Arab man married a Shona woman and lived among his in-laws. The man, who used to wear a skullcap called *chiremba* in Shona, later died. His children were called VaRemba to indicate their father's religious/cultural practice of wearing a skullcap. In other words, VaRemba are descendants of a man who wore a *chiremba*," says Mr Hamandishe.

Interestingly, Abrimosh Mohammed, who I met in Arusha, Tanzania, told me the skullcap is called *kilembe* in the Kiswahili language. I can't help seeing a similarity between *chiremba* and *kilembe*.

The VaRemba's totem is *zhou/nzou* (*ndlovu*) - elephant. An elephant is said to resemble a shrew mouse, with its long nose. The Arab man's nose, as indeed was the case with his children's, was longer than is generally the case with an African nose. The choice of the totem of an elephant was perhaps influenced by this physical characteristic.

The VaRemba belong to the following groups: VaDumha, VaTonga, VaNyakavi and VaSariri. Today they use various surnames such as Musoni,

Beta, Zhou, Mbeva, Surungwani, (or Silingwana in Ndebele), Makotore, Muzhinga, Hamandishe, Seremani, Mutangadura, Murimazhira, Foroma, Senderai, Zindoga, Mupanganyama, Mhizha, Katerere and Chissungo. The VaRemba are found in various areas of Zimbabwe, particularly in the east and south, for example: Mutoko (Katerere), Manicaland (Beta), Gutu (Hamandishe), Buhera (Makotore), Mberengwa (Zhou, Shurungwani and Seremani), Hwedza (Mutangadura in Zviyambi area) and Mount Darwin (Chisunga).

Hamandishe, also known as Mapanganyama, was a prominent man under Chief Gutu. He was killed by the Ndebele at Gondwi, between Chatsworth and Gutu. The present Hamandishe, my interviewee, is a counsellor (*gurukota*) for the present Chief Gutu, a Makuvaza.

During *Mfecane*, some of the VaRemba in Mberengwa fled to the Venda area of South Africa. When the security situation improved, some of them trekked back to settle in Mberengwa, where they are still to be found under Chief Mposi, who was a tributary chief under the Ndebele.

To this day, some of the VaRemba adhere to cultural practices that point to an Arab origin. Circumcision is one example, particularly in the Chinyika area of Gutu and Nyajena in Zaka. When pressed for reasons why circumcision is practised, the answer, invariably, is: "it is our tradition".

Even during the liberation war, the VaRemba of the Gutu area were provided with policemen to guard over them during the period of seclusion. The boys going for circumcision are called *madzinga*. The ritual itself is called *kudzingira*. The common greeting during the circumcision period is *saramariko*. I wish you well or peace be unto you. *Salama* (corrupted to *sarama* in Shona) in Kiswahili means well, or peace.

A story is told of Chief Dliso Mkhwananzi who could not father an heir. A MuRemba *inyanga* provided herbal treatment until the chief's wife conceived. The child was named Madzingire, later corrupted by the Ndebele to Majinkila. He later fathered Ngungumbane.

Apparently, this is not the first time that the Mkhwananzis had contact with VaRemba. Mhabahaba Mkhwananzi, the chief of Intunta village, was sent away by King Mzilikazi for his role in installing Nkulumane. Contrary to popular belief that Mhabahaba Mkhwananzi was killed alongside Gundwane Ndiweni and others, he was actually spared and given a few head of cattle. He went to live among the VaRemba in Mberengwa until his death and internment at Mutuzungwe (Nyathi, 2000).

The VaRemba do not eat pork and rabbit meat. As a general rule, they don't keep dogs. As one would expect, they won't eat a shrew mouse *(mudeme* or *mutswiri)*.

They will not partake of beef from a beast slaughtered by other people. When a circumcised MuRemba (who is presumed to be ritually clean) slaughters a beast he faces east. The holy city of Mecca is located in that direction. During the process, the man who slaughters the beast utters the following words: *"Bis Milayi Takabira"*. This compares with *Bismillahi, Allahu Akbar*, which means "I slaughter in the name of God, God is great!" Beef from a beast so slaughtered is said to be *halla*.

The VaRemba practice partial endogamy, a MuRemba man generally marrying the daughter of another MuRemba.

Links have been established and maintained with the outside Moslem world, especially Pakistan, Saudi Arabia and Egypt. Delegates from some of these countries have visited Gutu, Chinyika, and Chiguhunhle, where mosques have been established. Such visits have been reciprocated by some VaRemba from Zimbabwe.

Some VaRemba continue to give their children names that are derived from the Arabic language, for example. Muhamat, Seremani, and Saiyidi Mwenyi.

Customs that lead to burial disputes

For three weeks a wife's corpse has been lying in the hospital mortuary. Her people will not bury her. The husband and his people dare not proceed with the burial. They fear the dire consequences of a unilateral burial. Meanwhile, the deceased wife's close relatives are demanding a large herd of cattle and a staggering sum of money.

From time to time newspapers carry such a story, which can astound those not familiar with Shona customs.

To fully appreciate the ramifications of the social problem, one needs to understand the principles relating to family, spirituality, death, marriage, status of a wife and the deep seated fear of an avenging spirit (*ngozi/uzimu*). Marriage among traditional Africans goes beyond a contract between two spouses. It involves several families, on both sides. The knot is also tied by their spiritual families. On that basis, live-in or unofficial marriages can lead to problems.

A man intending to marry a woman appoints a go-between, *munyayi/umkhongi,* who approaches his future in-laws. Certain payments must be made before the marriage is formalised.

Among the Shona of Zimbabwe, the first payment of preliminary charges is called *zvibinge*. The prospective in-laws require a payment in order to facilitate discussions, called *vhuramuromo*, literally 'opening one's mouth'.

Usually, the prospective in-laws invite their close relatives to witness and participate in the marriage negotiations. The future son-in-law is charged a goat to be eaten by the participants. The goat is called *mbudzi yedare* (Interview with Lawrence Jenjezwa, 2000).

The prospective in-laws want to know how the intending husband got to know about their daughter. So, the future son-in-law is charged some money called *makandinzwa nani*.

When a foetus, the prospective bride would have kicked in her mother's womb. For those uncomfortable kicks, the future son-in-law must pay *mapfukudza dumbu*. This payment also used to be called *husha dzamai*. This was in reference to pieces of cloth tied around the waist in the belief that they would restore the womb to its usual position following delivery.

For the discomfort suffered by the woman's father when she pulled on his beard as a child, the future son-in-law must pay *matekenya ndebvu*.

Even the conjugal act must be paid for. The baby girl was a product of love-making during which the mother lay facing up. For that, the future son-in-law pays *mafunira mudenga* or *maverenga nhungo (ikubala intungo)* (Interview with Lawrence Jenjezwa, 2000).

These preliminary payments contrast with the traditional practice among the Ndebele, where such payments were not known. However, similar payments, such as *isivulamlomo* and *ukungaziwe*, for 'opening one's mouth' and 'getting to know' are finding their way into Ndebele society.

Lobola proper, known as *roora*, follows thereafter. It consists of cattle payments known as *danga* and *rusambo/rutsambo*, or *rugaba* as known among the Kalanga.

It is sometimes the non-payment of these charges that leads to a breakdown in discussions following a woman's death.

Roora, and associated payments, are due whether the wife is dead or alive. The in-laws will, under normal circumstances, remind the son-in-law about outstanding *roora* if the wife should die before the dues are settled in full. The son-in-law should then promise to pay the balance, *masadzirwa* or *masadziwa*.

When the promise is made, the deceased wife's relatives will sanction the burial. Burial of a wife must always be given the nod by the wife's blood relatives. The wife, though married, still belongs to her original family. It is they who have full authority over the corpse of their daughter.

The grave site is marked off by the deceased wife's relatives. One person, of her *mutopo* (totem), should, using a pick, mark the position of the grave. This is called *kutema rukarwa*. Unless one of her relatives performs the rite, burial will not take place.

None of the deceased wife's children can perform the *kutema rukarwa* rite. Her children have a different totem from their mother. They belong to the husband's people, whose totem they have adopted.

The wife's status is further reinforced by principles relating to spiritual possession. A woman can only be possessed by a spirit of her own *mutopo*. In spiritual terms, therefore, the wife belongs to her original family.

Among the Ndebele, separation and incorporation rites affect the wife's status. For example, she is buried according to her husband's people's burial rites.

Like other African people, the Shona believe in the hereafter. A person is regarded as having two shadows - the physical, that is visible, and the white shadow (*munhu*). "In fact, the spirits of the dead are so much part of Shona life that they can aptly be called spirit elders, the senior members of the community who now act as spirits" (Bourdillion, 1976).

African religious philosophy posits that there are good and bad spirits. An angered spirit can cause death. If the husband caused his wife's death, an avenging spirit wreaks havoc among the husband's people. Such a spirit does not confine its wrath to the nuclear family of the husband. Instead, it attacks the wider family. For example, married daughters may get divorced.

The husband's people dare not bury a 'foreigner' (*mutorwa*) lest she turns into a *chimwanakadzi*, an avenging spirit. This fear may lead to 'extortion' by the deceased wife's relatives.

Sometimes the relatives of the dead woman will agree to proceed with the burial of their daughter where not all lobola had been paid. The in-laws may, however, refuse to perform the rite, known as *kuparadza nhumbi (ukuchitha impahla)*, of 'scattering' the deceased clothes. It should be realised that all the deceased wife's property belongs to her people. It is they who will share their daughter's belongings. It is up to them to give some of the items to the children – but they are not obliged to do so.

If the in-laws refuse to perform the *kuparadza nhumbi* rite, the implication is that, should her former husband remarry, the spirit of the deceased wife may chase the new wife away.

So, under what conditions would the in-laws refuse to bury their daughter? This will happen in live-in marriages, *ukutshaya amapoto*, that have not been formalised traditionally. A more common instance is where a husband is thought to be responsible for his wife's death. A troublesome husband, *murume anoshusha*, may drive his wife to commit suicide. The in-laws would argue that, if he no longer loved his wife, he should have given her some *gupuro* and taken her back to her people.

Alternatively, a go-between may be used to return the wife to her people. In this case too, some *gupuro* must be taken along, as a symbol to the wife's aunt that their niece has been rejected. A verbal rejection has no formal status. On payment of a fine, the husband may reverse his decision.

"Is the demand for a large herd of cattle warranted?" I pose the question to Mr Jenjezwa.

The answer is quick in coming. "Yes. You see, *roora* is not meant to be paid in full. The husband's family only needs to pay a little to signal acceptance. In fact, the in-laws don't expect a *mukuwasha* (son-in-law) to settle in full.

"Yes, the mother's beast, *mombe yamai*, must be paid. The father's dues will come in due course. After all *mukwambo mutoko (umkhwenyana yinxoza)*," says Mr Jenjezwa in defence of the age-old Shona customary practice, likening a son-in-law to bark fibre, you exploit him at all times.

Nothing unusual in demanding cellphone

The cellphone craze has gripped Zimbabwe. The cellphone is so sought after that is has entered the realm of the traditional custom of lobola. A Harare man was reported as having demanding a cellphone from his prospective son-in-law, whose family were taken aback by what they considered to be an outrageous demand. The intransigence of the man threatened to scuttle the marriage negotiations. His close relatives eventually prevailed over him and he reluctantly abandoned his demand for a cellphone.

The lobola-cellphone matter generated lively debate in many social circles. Was the Harare man reasonable or not?

Pamela Reynolds and Collen Crawford Cousins, in their book entitled *'Lwaano Lwanyika,* Tonga Book of the Earth', define lobola or bride wealth as "marriage payment from one family to another to secure rights for a husband over a woman's labour, the right to control her movements, rights to her sexuality and her children."

Alternatively, lobola could be viewed as an economic transaction between the male parties and a means through which a man appropriated the means of production.

The payment of lobola is done in full recognition that a woman plays a pivotal role in wealth creation. Other than providing labour herself, she also bears children who contribute much needed labour. And the woman was the producer of producers. The young woman would, on getting married, bring more wealth to the family in the form of lobola payments.

Among the Ndebele, when a girl reached puberty, it was often said *"Izinkomo sezilunguzile"* (lobola cattle are expected anytime).

The similarity between the words lobola (Ndebele) and *roora* (Shona) suggest the existence of the practice before the two languages developed separately. Lobola as a concept must be centuries old, however, what is paid as lobola has been changing over time.

For example, a long time ago the Tonga worked the hard and dry soils of the Zambezi valley using wooden hoes. This was a gruelling experience. These hoes were likely to have been highly valued, but hard to obtain because iron was scarce in the valley. By the nineteenth century, the Tonga were exchanging ivory and slaves and even, so travellers said, their children for iron hoes (Reynolds and Cousins, 1993).

Because of its value, the hoe was an essential item of bride wealth and was one of the symbols of a leader's power. The iron hoes used by the Tonga were made by the Nambiya and called *maamba acidenda*. Implements such as hoes were used by other Bantu groups, including the Shona. With the introduction of livestock such as goats, sheep and cattle, lobola payment was made with these animals. Cattle, especially, came to dominate the scene from far back in history until the present time. The importance of cattle lies in their economic and social value. The second half of the nineteenth century saw the introduction of artefacts of European origin. Hunters and traders brought these items to exchange for ivory, feathers, gold and fur. At Old Bulawayo, white traders set up permanent settlements. The new items heralded a new era in the material culture of the people. Cloth, for example, was beginning to replace leather as dress material. Metal containers replaced gourds and earthenware pots.

The introduction of such substitute items had a disastrous effect on local industries. Among the Ndebele, the skin tanning and pottery industries collapsed. By the nineteenth century, Portuguese traders, such as Joao Ferreira, Mendonca and Leronco Monteiro, among others, introduced cloth to the Tonga. Prior to this, the Tonga used to grow cotton and had weaving industries that turned cotton into blankets and items of clothing.

Some of the new artefacts became part of lobola payment. Today a son-in-law is required to buy his father-in-law an overcoat (*ijazi*) and a blanket (*ingubo*); a shawl (*lema* in Kalanga) for the mother-in-law. These were trade items that came into the country before colonisation. A water jug (*ibhuleki*) is usually one of the items used as lobola payment. Interestingly, these are now accepted as traditional as if they had always been part of the payment.

After colonisation, new demands were made on the son-in-law. The expectation is that the father-in-law is to be given a suit, a pair of shoes and a hat. The mother-in-law also demands a two-piece suit, hat and shoes. These items have become accepted as part and parcel of the lobola tradition.

It needs to be pointed out that the introduction of these items did raise eyebrows among some members of society at the time. They did not understand why items of foreign origin were being demanded as lobola payment. The Nguni element in Zimbabwe has generally been reluctant to introduce new items.

Now comes the demand for a cellphone, and people scream! This is history repeating itself. Attacking the demand for cellphones is misdirecting one's energies. What ought to be attacked, and relentlessly too, is the concept of lobola. The practice, as indeed is the case with several other 'traditional customs', is incompatible with the drive for gender equality.

THE KALANGA

The Tjikalanga speaking people, or Bakalanga, are found in south–western Zimbabwe. They are also found in northern and north-western Botswana. It seems that the Tjikalanga speaking area used to be much bigger than it is today. In the north-west they were in contact with the Tonga of the Leya dialect. Research has shown that they were also found in Nkayi and Lupane (Nyathi, unpublished, Alexander et al, 2000).

The Kalanga belong to the Leopard's Kopje culture that was based in the Khami area, west of present day Bulawayo. The Kalanga have been in the south-western and western areas of Zimbabwe for over a thousand years.

The advent of the Ndebele in 1839/40 began the reduction of the Kalanga speaking area. Some Kalanga were incorporated into the various villages. Ndebele chiefs were appointed over them and the situation has not changed to this day.

Examples of Ndebele chieftaincies among the Kalanga abound –Emphandeni (Chief Mpofu), Osabeni (Chief Ndiweni), Kwezimnyama (Chief Ndiweni), Dliwampando (Chief Jiyane) and Emagogweni (Chief Sithole).

Even before the arrival of the Ndebele, the Kalanga had been overrun by the Torwa who were coming from the collapsing Great Zimbabwe State. The Torwa State, based in western Zimbabwe, was founded by Mukwati and Torwa. The arrival of the people from the Zimbabwe State introduced stone building culture in the areas formerly occupied by the Kalanga.

Kalanga tradition remembers their first king as Tjibundule (Tshibundule). He was also known as Hundumuro or Chihundumuro. He was the last Mutapa to rule over the people that we today call Shona. Tjibundule was defeated by Dombodzvuku, who had solicited assistance from Tumbare (Bhebhe), towards the close of the seventeenth century. The Kalanga came under the hegemony of the Rozvi Mambos. Some of the Rozvi became an integral part of Kalanga society.

The colonial era further reduced the Kalanga speaking areas. The Kalanga themselves were evicted from areas that had hitherto been part of the peripheral or tributary Ndebele State. They were evicted from areas such as Figtree, Marula, Leighwoods, Soluswe and Somnene.

When the Ndebele were evicted from the core Ndebele State, they were pushed into former Kalanga areas, including Tsholotsho, Kezi and Wenlock. This marked the second incorporation of the Kalanga that took place in the colonial period. The Kalanga in the affected areas lost their language and started speaking Ndebele. When the colonial government recognised Shona and Ndebele as national languages, Tjikalanga suffered yet another blow. Tjikalanga belongs to the same language group as Shona and Nambiya. The Kalanga language has dialects including Lilima, Talawunda and Jawunda. Kalanga society has, for many centuries, incorporated groups of people coming from the east, south and west. The Torwa came from the east, while the following came from the south: the Kwena from Tswapong in Botswana, the Birwa – especially the Serumula and Sikoba Merola houses - from the north-western part of Limpopo Province, the Venda, the Hurutshe and Pedi from South Africa.

A close look at Kalanga society will reveal quieter south-north migrations preceding the more calamitous *Mfecane* movements of the early nineteenth century. Some groups came from as far south as present day Lesotho and KwaZulu-Natal.

Today the Kalanga of Zimbabwe are found in Bulilima-Mangwe, Tsholotsho and Matobo districts. Their language is now hardly taught and, where it is, only up to Grade 3. Lobbying is underway to empower the so-called minority languages, which include Kalanga, Venda, Tonga, Nambiya, Sotho and Shangane.

The origin of the name Kalanga

Where did the word Kalanga come from? The Portuguese asked that question as far back as the sixteenth century about the people they called the Mokarangas, who called themselves Vakaranga. Some historians believe the name Kalanga means 'people of the sun'. East of Lake Tanganyika there was a land referred to as *ukuranga*, and its people as *wakaranga*. Among those people *ukuranga* meant the land of the people of the sun. In their language *ilanga* meant the sun.

Other historians believe otherwise, arguing that in the Kalanga or Karanga language, *ukaranga* means the son of a young wife or little root. Posselt (1935) argues that the offspring of junior wives of paramount rulers may have been called *vakaranga* (Wentzel, 1983). Posselt does not see any relationship between the word *vakaranga* and the sun.

Others, starting from the Karanga/Kalanga language itself, argue that *vakaranga* means the punishers, derived from the verb *kuranga*, which means to punish. In an interview with Saul Gwakuba Ndlovu in 2000, he concurred with this view, stating that the term Kalanga derives from the practice of Chief Tjibundule of disciplining his people by beating them with a stick on the back. The term *ilanga* in the language which Tjibundule's people spoke meant 'to discipline'. His people referred to his residence as Kalanga, that is, the place of the one who disciplines with a stick. Paul R. Dube explains that the 'ka' is the locative morpheme, while 'langa' is a verb stem used as a proper noun, hence the word Kalanga.

Aeneas Chigwedere (1980) agrees with the 'people of the sun' theory. He states that the term Karanga referred to the Dziva (Siziba) or Hungwe (Nyoni) group, which embraces the Nguni and Sotho or Tswana, in whose language *langa* means sun. He further argues that these people moved south, from the Nile Valley region, ahead of the present day Shona. Interestingly, among the Ndebele, who are of Nguni stock, the sun has important significance. The King is symbolised by the sun and is usually referred to as the sun. King Mzilikazi Khumalo is well known for the words uttered when he discovered that Prince Nkulumane had been installed King, *"Aliko ilanga elingaphuma elinye lingakatshoni"* (There is no sun that rises before the other sets). When King Lobengula Khumalo fled north in 1893 those of his people following him were told *"ilanga selitshonile"* (the sun has set). They were being advised to go back and surrender to the pursuing whites. Among Mzilikazi Khumalo's praises are the following lines:

Inkwenkwezi and 'elesilimela'
Ilanga eliphuma endlebeni yendlovu laphuma amakwezi abikelana.

In the past, the Zulu and their offshoot, the Ndebele, built their homes facing the sun, which to them was a symbol of power, authority and rejuvenation. Research at koBulawayo (Old Bulawayo) has found that King Lobengula's residence (the royal enclosure) faced east and north, not west as has become the general practice in Matabeleland today.

Kalanga inheritance

Succession and inheritance are vexing issues that all peoples of the world have grappled with at some time. Each group has, over the years, developed a set of rules and guidelines that govern such matters. The Kalanga are no exception.

Among the Kalanga, the oldest son by the first wife may not have been the one who succeeded his father as chief. The senior wife was not necessarily the one who was married first, she was the one who was betrothed to the chief first. The chief was succeeded by his first son by his senior wife, who is referred to in Kalanga as *nlongo buta*. The term means literally the sleeping bride. It should be noted that the custom applied to ordinary people and royalty. The son of the *nlongo buta* was the chief inheritor of his late father's estate. Other women married much earlier than her were bound to respect her irrespective of how much younger she might have been.

The arrangement was entered into by the parents of the chief-to-be and the parents of the young girl. At times, such an arrangement was reached even before the girl was born. The girl was thus born into and bound by arrangements made long before her birth. Wife seniority among the Kalanga was very similar to that among the Ndebele. The eldest son by the eldest wife was not necessarily the future King. There were two conditions that determined royal succession. The son must have been born of a King. In essence, this meant that any sons born before he became King did not qualify for the royal throne. Mzilikazi Khumalo had at least four sons before he became King - Mangwana, Muntu (known as Tshukisa), Qalingaana and Lopila. Secondly, the senior wife was one born of a king of a friendly tribe. In 1879 King Lobengula Khumalo dispatched Lotshe Hlabangane, chief of Induba village, to find him a wife who would bear the future king. Her name was Xhwalile, the daughter of King Mzila Nxumalo of the Shangani nation.

The people who are called the Kalanga comprise members of several ethnic groups. The Venda from across the Limpopo River arrived in the nineteenth century and were incorporated into Kalanga society. Included in this group are the Malaba people. Various Sotho and Tswana groups have also been incorporated. The Hurutshe (Khurutsi), that is the Shaba or Nshaba, have also become Kalanga. Domboshaba at Kalakamate in Botswana is named after them.

The Babirwa, the ethnic group to which this writer belongs, moved from South Africa into Botswana where they got entangled with the Talawunda

Kalanga. Once settled in Zimbabwe, in the first quarter of the nineteenth century, some Babirwa moved west into Bakalanga. The Babirwa claim to have raised a good breed of milk cows and the Kalanga flocked to their homes in search of milk. "*Mondayi?*" (Where are you going?) some Kalanga asked. "*Tondakunkala!*" (to a place where there is milk) responded the Kalanga who were on their way to ask for milk. The Babirwa came to be known as aBakaka in reference to the milk that they had in abundance (interview with Lot Mathiba Nyathi, 1982).

The Tswapong Kwena (Ngwenya) who came from Molepole (Mulepulule) trekked north and got absorbed by the Kalanga. The Pedi were another Sotho group that was similarly incorporated. The Khuphes belong to this group. There are a number of subdivisions of the Khuphe people, for example the Tjilalu and Ngwadi. Chief Nswazwi in the Mayitengwe area is head of the former group (interview with Saul Gwakuba Ndlovu, 2000).

This process of incorporation has been going on for centuries. The Torwa, who came from Great Zimbabwe, were amongst the earliest to be incorporated. The Rozvi (or Nyayi) came into the Kalanga area towards the close of the seventeenth century. The language spoken by the Rozvi differed considerably from the Kalanga. The Rozvi could converse in the company of the Kalanga and would not be understood. In their speech they used *bodo* to mean no, as spoken in some parts of Masvingo.

The Tonga are recognised as having preceded the Kalanga in settling in western Zimbabwe. Sanzukwi, in Bulilima South, bears testimony to this assertion. Sanzukwi, claims Saul Gwakuba Ndlovu, refers to an expert in honey culture. Mpandamatenga is another Tonga word, meaning the one who cracks the sky. There are several other surviving Tonga names all over Matabeleland and Mashonaland, for example Dongamuzi, Nkayi, Lupane and Kadoma.

The Tonga found the San who they did not completely incorporate or chase away. The Kalanga found and enslaved some of them. It was common to hear a Kalanga man say "*Nkwa wangu wandakapfuwaa*" (My San who I am looking after). These captive San people adopted Kalanga totems and intermarried.

How the Nyubi tackled epidemics

A man walks into my office and introduces himself as belonging to an ethnic group closely related to the Kalanga - the Nyubi. They have occupied the Matopo Hills for several centuries. He wishes to have some of the group's traditions recorded.

The Matopos represents an area where man has developed a close relationship with nature. This seems to have happened at two levels. The first level relates to the hilly nature of the Matopos. The people of the area say that 'rock has sustenance', *'Piyanedombo. Dombo linetshilenga'*. The area south of the Matopos is arid. However, the Matopos is better watered. The numerous rocks collect water and direct it towards the nearby fields. More water percolates into the soil than would have been the case if the rocks were not there. The area also has a wide variety of fruit. Living in the Matopo Hills increases your chances of adequate sustenance.

Several groups from the south trekked north and settled among the hills. Sebola (Sibhula) and his people, of Sotho origin, are a good example. They arrived in the Matopo Hills before the Ndebele and became incorporated into Nyubi society. Some of their descendents are found in the Lukadzi-Sotshe area.

At another level, the Nyubi had a number of shrines. Dula (KoMaswabi) and Njelele are two outstanding examples. Generally, the two shrines specialised in matters of war, dealing with pests, *ubudli*, such as locusts, and animals like baboons and leopards. They were also involved in the eradication of epidemics. Some of the epidemics that come to mind are *indalimana* (rinderpest) of 1896 and *ifuleza* (influenza) that broke out at the close of the First World War.

The Njelele shrine was also used for rain ceremonies. There were other shrines, *amadaka*, like Zhilo, koMavumbuka Ncube, Kumbudzi, koDabha Ncube or Magubu, and Dondoriya, which also concentrated on rain ceremonies.

I will now focus on how the Nyubi dealt with epidemics. Two short pegs, *izikhonkwane*, were driven into the ground on opposite sides of a flowing river. The plant used is called *isikhukhukhu* in the Ndebele language. Fibre from the same plant was used to join the two pegs.

The people gathered on one side of the river. On the opposite side, next to the second peg, a winnowing basket, *ukhomane*, was placed. The basket contained porridge.

The officiating man stood in the centre of the flowing river. In his hand he held a broken gourd, *ukubachela*, which contained a medicinal concoction. His other hand clutched a leafy branch of *umsehla* tree. It was used in place of a flywhisk, *itshoba*. The people proceeded to cross the stream in such a manner that the string was between the legs of the one crossing, *ukuxamalazela intambo*.

Meanwhile, the official sprayed those crossing with the medicine. Those crossing were instructed not to look back, *ukunyemukula*. On crossing the river, each person took some of the porridge with his or her left hand. The first mouthful was spat onto the ground. The second and subsequent mouthfuls were swallowed.

This done, he or she proceeded home without looking back. When all the people had undergone the ritual, the winnowing basket was collected by the official. The basket was then hung from an *isigangatsha* tree by string. The swinging basket faced all directions. In the process, so goes the belief, the basket collected the epidemic from all around.

During the ritual the people abstained from sex. Further, salt was not added to any food. After collecting the basket, the official would either stay in a village or sleep in the bush. The basket was returned to the owner.

The final part of the ritual consisted of symbolically stopping or 'closing' the epidemic. This was done by a separate group of people. They too had to abstain from all sexual activities and were not allowed to eat salted food. This group looked for a special 'O' shaped hole in a rock. The hole needed to be very deep. There is one such hole on Hwariyahwadzi Mountain, a short distance from Dula Mountain.

The assumption was that the swinging basket used during the *zhambuko* (the ritual of crossing the stream) collected the epidemic and channelled it into this deep hole. Using stones, the hole was closed, and, by so doing, the epidemic was sealed off.

Rain–making ceremonies are part of African culture

Rain-making ceremonies have been part of African culture since time immemorial. There is an underlying belief that spiritual intervention can result in the heavens opening up.

Kings performed rituals to cause the rains to fall. For example, King Lobengula went into the goat byre to perform the solemn rite. During that period no guns were to be fired. Armies were not to be sent out on raids. Anything red was not to be exposed in the open.

Among the Shona and related groups rain–making shrines abounded. There was a hierarchy of these ranging from national to local shrines. Local shrines went by various names such as *Daka* or *Mtolo*. Njelele is the best known national shrine.

The Chronicle of January 20, 2001, reported Chief Hwange as saying that people from his area used to go to Njelele to request for rains. There were established routes that they followed. He was attributing train derailments in the area to failure to recognise these routes.

The rain-making rituals were performed just before the start of the rainy season. When *amawosana* came back from Njelele, rains came to erase their footprints, *ukucitsha izinyawo zabo*.

When the rains failed to fall, measures were taken to seek spiritual intervention so that the rains would come. The rites, it was believed, resulted in cloud formation and induced the clouds so formed to release the rain.

When the dry spell persisted, elders in a given locality took steps to bring the spell to an end. The 2000-2001 rainy season, particularly dry in Matabeleland South, was no exception. Unfortunately, the rituals performed were to no avail. I caught up with one of the senior elders who briefed me on the rituals that they performed.

According to Menyezwa Nyathi, a ritual known as *ukwebula inxoza* (barking a tree) was performed. In cultural terms, Sankonjana, also known as Babirwa, is a melting pot. Ndebele, Birwa (or Sotho) and Kalanga traditions co-exist. The term *ukwebula inxoza* is Ndebele. However, the people at Sankonjana also call the ritual *tenhela,* the Kalanga rendition of the same rite. The elders assess the situation and if, in their view, the weather pattern warrants spiritual intervention, they will initiate the ritual.

At Sankonjana, this privilege falls on the shoulders of men like Nyumbana Driver Dube and Menyeza Nyathi. Once the intention to perform the ritual was made known, the local chief, Lemakatso Silebuho Nyathi, was approached. He summoned his subjects to a *phutheho* (meeting) at his *kgtla* (court).

The words *phutheho* and *kgtla* bear testimony to the presence of the Birwa influences in the area. The Birwa originally came from Botswana, especially the areas of Bubonong, Gobajangu and Semolala – what today is known as the Madinare area on the north of north-eastern Botswana. Some came straight from the north-western Transvaal (Limpopo Province).

On the appointed day, men gathered at the foothills of Sankonjana Mountain. Kafusi River flows close by. When the men arrived at the selected spot, they piled up all their knobkerries (*induku*) in one place. One man obtained some bark fibre (*ingxoza*) with which to tie all the knobkerries into a single bundle. Another man picked up the bundle and threw it to the ground. Dogs milled around, itching to participate in the impending hunt.

One of the officiating elders reminded the participants of the regulations to be observed. All those setting forth from the meeting point should return to the same spot. No one is allowed to desert during the hunt. No one should carry money on his person, nor bring salt with which to season the meat.

Elderly members of the community such as Bheka, Marko Siziba, Nyumbana Dube and Meyezwa remained behind. Their frail bodies would not allow them to undertake the gruelling journey through mountains and valleys.

Those proceeding on the hunt looked out for exposed animal bones They buried such bones. The men also removed cobwebs they found on trees. They also looked for trees that had been struck by lightning. These trees were tied with a creeper known as *isibhobhono*. Wood was collected and piled around the trees, which were then burnt to ashes. Any animals that they came across were killed, including tortoises and leguans. In the afternoon the hunting party went back to the starting point. A big fire made by the elders welcomed them. Animals killed during the hunt were skinned and their flesh roasted. No salt was used in seasoning the meat. In groups, the men ate the roasted meat. Bones and skins from the animals were thrown into the fire.

Dzibalevula usibone
Mbedzi nkulu

This incantation by one of the elders is a reference to Mwali at Njelele. The appeal was rendered in both the Kalanga and Ndebele languages. The smell of the smoke from the burning bones is said to please Mwali, who causes the rain to fall.

After partaking of the meat, the men washed their hands and legs in the nearby Kafusi River. If there was plenty of water, the men washed their entire bodies.

Should the rains fail to follow, another date was fixed. In this particular case, the rains did not fall. A severe drought continued to grip the area. Women also had a role to play in the rain ritual. Adult women gathered together and beat drums as they danced. In the past, they went about bare breasted and with no cover on their heads. The women went to the foothills of Sankonjana Mountain. There they danced until the men arrived from the hunt.

In the ritual, an announcement was made to the women, informing them how many animals their menfolk had managed to kill. Part of the roasted meat was given to the women. With the ritual over, both men and women retired to their homes. No one was allowed to take a piece of meat home. With great expectation, the men and women gazed into the sky in hope that the heavens would open up. If not today, perhaps tomorrow.

Mbanje originally entwined with culture

"THERE are a lot more stories that I did not tell you last time," exclaims Nyumbana Dube of Sankonjana. His face that has defied the ravages of time breaks into a broad smile.

"Did I tell you how the whites came into this country?" he inquires. He goes on to narrate how Zimbabwe was colonised. "And have you heard about Mgandane Dlodlo?" he asks, in between pinches of snuff. Though I admit I had heard about him, he goes on to narrate how the Ndebele hero of the 1893 Anglo-Ndebele war met his death. The whites from Fort Victoria (Masvingo) were able to identify him as a leader and shot him in cold blood. Indeed, I have listened to various versions of how Mgandane Dlodlo, chief of Inxa village, was killed by the whites. One very popular version says he was decapitated and had his severed genitals stuffed into his mouth.

The last story Nyumbana Dube tells me is about why the growth and consumption of mbanje *(insangu)* was prohibited in the Fort Usher area.

Ndebele men and women both took snuff. Traders and hunters coming into Matabeleland in the 1860s and 1870s left behind written records of how Ndebele women, particularly, used to pester them for *kwayi*. In those days, the best tobacco came from Chief Nyoka's people in the Gokwe area. However, tobacco or mbanje smoking was the preserve of men. "Smoking is indulged in by men and boys and its main object seems to be to provoke a strong flow of saliva" (Krige, 1977). The object was, surely, much more than the provocation of a strong flow of saliva. Mbanje gives the smoker a 'high'. It is said to give a soldier Dutch courage.

Mbanje is not indigenous to Africa. It has, however, found its way into the African religious sphere. For example, some people use it to scare away goblins, *imikhoba*, known as *ondofa*.

"In the past, when we went to pay homage at the Njelele shrine, we used to take with us several cat skins *(insimba)*, leaves of tobacco and some mbanje," says Lot Mathiba Nyathi during a group interview at Sankonjana.

Mbanje was smoked through the aid of a device known as *igudu*. "Mbanje is put into the bowl of a smoking horn *(igudu)* and a coal of fire is placed on the top of it. The horn is half filled with water, the mouth placed at the thick end of the horn and the smoke drawn through the water by deep inhalations from the chest producing frequent coughing all the time" (Krige, 1977).

Men used to take turns to inhale the smoke from *igudu*. The Ndebele saying *indaba esegudwini* (talking around the pipe) derives from the smoking sessions. The matter under discussion during smoking is *indaba esegudwini*. Herd boys used to engage in various games in the veld. Charles Celt Thomas, in his book, 'Thomas Morgan Thomas – Pioneer Missionary 1828 – 1884', describes one game that the boys engaged in. "At the edge of every pool or stream, large numbers of small clay cones could be seen in the water. They were an inch-and-half in length, tapering from half an inch to a point. They were made by rolling a small lump of clay between the palms of their hands.

"The little, or even the big, boys would sit at the edge of the water, each with a big lump of clay at his side, roll a cone, and then, holding it loosely in his curved fingers, toss it in the air with a spinning motion, the sharp point downwards. The object was to try and get the cone to enter the water without making a splash." (Courtesy of Dr JoAnn McGregor and Marieke Clarke).

I was to learn later that this particular game, popular in the past, was called *inyonganyonga* (interview with Hudson Halimana Ndlovu, 1999).

At times, the boys stole their father's mbanje and made their own version of *igudu* by the poolside. This version, according to Nyumbana Dube, was called *umbhansi*.

The boys made *umbhansi* by "... making two holes in the shape of the two sides of an inverted triangle and meeting at a point under the surface where a small earth bottle was formed for holding the water. The pipe was fitted in one of the holes and the reed in the other, and the substitution is complete" (Nyathi, 1970).

"Boys from Fort Usher used to look after Tshenisi's herds of cattle and took them to the water at the Rhodes Matopos Dam," says Nyumbana Dube. Tshenisi is the Ndebele name for the Chennells family who owned, until 1993, Honeydale Estate and Matopo Vale. "The land lay adjacent to the Matopos Agricultural Station and also to the Gulati Communal Areas." The land has since been bought by Harold Ndlovu, a retired headmaster (Ranger, 1999).

"Have you heard about that school at Sodoma?" asks Nyumbana Dube. I figure he is referring to the Rhodes Estate Preparatory School.

"When Tshenisi's herd boys got to the Rhodes Matopos Dam they made *umbhansi* and smoked some mbanje. Then one day, three white boys from the school at Sodoma visited the dam.

"Their attention was drawn to *umbhansi* on the dam's edge. They studied it closely and figured out it was an mbanje smoking device. Two of the boys, eager to get a lift, lit up the mbanje and started inhaling.

"There were several boats in the dam. The boys jumped into one boat and, soon thereafter, it capsized. The one who had not smoked mbanje went to report the death of his two colleagues.

"It was discovered that they had smoked mbanje. The district commissioner sent police over from the Fort Usher area advising the people to stop growing and smoking mbanje."

On that note our interview ended, with Nyumbana Dube inhaling deeply from his snuff box. So long Nkwite!

The Kalanga and 'Nholo we mwizana'

For the better part of a week, one issue dominated conversation in Bulawayo. In offices and commuter buses, at bus stops and on factory floors, the talk was about *nholo we mwizana*, an age old Kalanga cultural practice. Interest in the matter was generated by a story in the *Sunday News* about a woman from Kezi who burnt her father–in-law's hut in protest against his sexual advances.

One might have expected that most people in the region would be fairly au fait with both the history and customs of the Kalanga. Professor David Beach (1980) explains the situation as follows: "The position [of the Kalanga] between the better known states (Ndebele and Ngwato) and the peoples on either side of them has meant that they have been almost totally neglected historically, and so far there is virtually no traditional evidence available on the Kalanga that could illuminate their history before 1650, or indeed, before 1800."

Be that as it may, there is general consensus on the key elements of *nholo we mwizana*.

Nholo, in the Kalanga language, means head and *mwizana* a lamb. So, *nholo we mwizana* means head of a lamb. But what is the connection between the cultural practice and the head of a lamb?

"Very good that you ask that question," said Mr Raphael Jonathan Bhutshe. "My mother was a pure Kalanga. When a young man married, he was not allowed to have sexual intercourse with his wife before she was approved as a daughter-in-law by the family."

Approval by the family took the form of the father-in–law having sexual intercourse with the daughter-in-law. The relationship was engaged in on the first night following her arrival at her in-laws. The community accepted the practice.

"You see, Mr Pathisa, among the Balilima in Botswana, it was the opposite of what the Kalanga did. A young man marrying into a Lilima family was required to prove his manhood before he could take their daughter's hand in marriage. Mature girls in the family had sex with the prospective husband. If the young man's manhood passed the rigorous test, the future wife would not have grounds for deserting the husband because of his lack of sexual virility," said Mr Bhutshe.

Among the Kalanga, sexual intercourse between father-in-law and his daughter-in-law served as an initiation into the family.

Responding to a suggestion that the purpose of the one-off encounter was to test the girl's virginity, Mr Bhutshe had this to say.

"No, no. Virginity tests could be undertaken by women on their own without assistance from men. In any case, among the Kalanga, the daughter-in-law's loss of virginity was not a stigma. With or without her virginity, the daughter-in-law would still undergo *nholo we mwizana*," said Mr Bhutshe emphatically.

So what purpose did *nholo we mwizana* serve within a family? The Kalanga, like several other African ethnic groups, were strongly patriarchal. The man was the unchallenged head of the household. He presided over disputes among his charges. For the daughter-in-law who has had sexual intercourse with her father-in-law, all barriers are removed. She would report, without inhibition, any matter concerning her sexuality.

Another Kalanga tradition was that on the death of the head of the household, the eldest son could marry all his late father's wives – except his own mother. In the late 1920s my own family experienced this phenomenon when one of my grandfathers married his late father's youngest wife. Though originally Sotho, my people, by marrying Kalanga wives, ended up adopting some Kalanga cultural practices.

Such a practice helped to keep the wider family together. Younger wives did not, on the death of their husbands, have to go back to their own people.

The critical assumption here is that if a father has had sexual intercourse with his son's wife, the son, on the death of his father, could have unimpeded access to the widows.

Concerning the name of the practice, Mr Bhutshe explained as follows: "If the father is the head of the family, he is likened to a ram. The son is therefore likened to a small sheep, *mwizana*. In sexual matters the law of the jungle applied. The powerful monopolised access to sex. The powerful ram chased the small ones - *mwizana* - so that it could have the lion's share."

However, those asserting the virginity test theory explain it differently. The penis glans of the father is likened to a head - a big head. The son's is small – just like the *nholo we mwizana*. A small head, therefore, cannot test virginity. What is needed is a bigger head – which the father has – and it is ideal in testing for virginity.

However, according to Saul Gwakuba Ndlovu, it was only the Rozwi, incorporated into Kalanga society, who practiced the custom of *nholo we mwizana* and not the rest of the Kalanga people. In fact, other Kalanga groups such as the Lilima regarded it as a taboo. The custom of *nholo we mwizana* rested on the principle that a chief begets a chief. The reigning chief fathers a child in place of his son, so that the eldest 'son' is actually the progeny of his 'grandfather'. Only the first born son is fathered in this manner. The rest, who do not become chiefs, are not fathered by the reigning chief – their grandfather.

Once again, the custom compares with the Ndebele idea that a king is born of a king. The difference lies in the arrangements made to effect the custom.

Fortson Badiman Dube maintains that there was another main reason behind the *nholo we mwizana* cultural practice. Dube is the son of Chief Masendu who had thirty-six wives. Dube was born when the chief was over seventy years of age. The late chief's first three wives went through the practice. When Chief Masendu married his fourth wife the custom had fallen into disuse. That was sometime in the 1930s.

According to Dube, the custom, which should not be called *nholo we mwizana*, was practised in order to test whether the daughter-in-law had pulled her labia. The pulling of the labia was believed to stimulate the husband during sexual intercourse.

A Kalanga man wishing to marry did not go to his future in-laws for formal introduction – *ukuuvela* as is practised among the Ndebele. The bride was smuggled out of her home at night. The family of the bride would then be advised to *hakelayi*, look this way for your daughter.

On the first night, the father-in-law had sexual intercourse with his daughter-in-law with the sole purpose of determining whether or not she had her labia pulled.

The onus of pulling the labia fell on the aunt to whom the girl had been attached. Each daughter was attached to an aunt. The aunt's husband could, if he so wished, marry his wife's niece. However, if the aunt's husband did not marry his wife's niece, any boy could marry her. This is the aunt who shouldered all the blame if she neglected one of her responsibilities to her brothers' daughter.

The responsibilities of paying lobola fell on the father and not the son. If he discovered his daughter-in-law had unpulled labia, he paid lobola in the form of hornless cattle, *ngombe ye gumu*.

When the bride's parents saw the hornless beasts, they immediately knew what that meant. The father's sister had reneged on her responsibility. The aunt was summoned and strongly admonished for her sin of omission.

It was at this point that *nholo we mwizana* occurred. The bride's father was expected to slaughter one of the beasts. The groom and his father partook of the meat, as did the aunt, her husband and the brides' parents. Inevitably some neighbours were invited.

A *mwizana*, as opposed to a *mwiza*, a full grown sheep, does not have horns. The pulled labia resemble horns. Hornless beasts thus resemble unpulled labia, a shameful condition of the daughter.

Like many African cultural practices, *nholo we mwizana* has fallen into disuse under the onslaught of Christianity and modernisation. This is not to say the practice died out at the same time everywhere. Pockets of resistance still exist to this day - hence the much talked about *Sunday News* story.

Observance of traditional holy days

An article appeared in the *Sunday News* about two Seventh Day Adventist Church members being reported by a neighbourhood watch committee in Nkayi for failing to observe a traditional rest day.

The weekly rest day, which is never the same in all areas of Zimbabwe, is called *chisi* in Shona. There does not seem to be an Ndebele equivalent for this day. In the Nguni world, the observance only exists through contact with the Kalanga, who have come to observe the day.

However, this should not create an impression that the Nguni did not observe a holy day. The day when there was no moon was regarded as a holy day and no agricultural activities were undertaken. Nor did *izinyanga* work on this day.

Chisi is a religious phenomenon connected with the Shona-Kalanga-Nambiya world. *Chisi* should, therefore, be understood as an environmental ideology hammered out on the anvil of the relationship between religion and conservation. Professor Terence Ranger in his book, *Voices from the Rocks*, quotes Michael Ncube, formerly of Hlekwini, who says: "Njelele used to lay down everything – when to plant, when to eat certain plants, when to reap..."

Matabeleland South, including Tsholotsho, Bubi, and parts of Nkayi and Lupane in Matabeleland North observe Wednesday as a *chisi*. These seem to be the areas that come under the direct influence and control of Njelele. In the Gokwe area, where the Nevana spirit medium holds sway, the day of rest is Thursday. During the time of King Lobengula, Nevana was referred to as *Salukazana,* or *Salgazana* in some colonial literature. The Jambezi area in Hwange also observes Thursdays.

Wonder Kuimba of Mashonaland West reports that, in his area, which is under the influence of the spirit medium of Nyamuswa, Thursday is observed as a holy day. Nyamuswa's area of influence covers Makonde, Hurungwe and Chinhoyi. Mashonaland Central, according to Christopher Chihota, observes Friday as a holy day. The spirit medium of Kasvamundzira (in charge of Bindura) and Matope (in charge of Mount Darwin) among others, control this. David Dumbuka from Gutu says they observe Thursdays as holy days. However, in the past, it used to be Wednesday.

From Manicaland, Charles Maunze says some parts of the province observe Wednesdays. A survey of the whole country seems to indicate that the holy days are either Wednesdays, Thursdays or Fridays. In my limited research, I did not come across an area that observes Mondays, Tuesdays, Saturdays or Sundays as holy days. While the holy days differ from place to place, there is agreement as to the prohibitions associated with the day. On the chosen holy day, communities were prohibited from undertaking agricultural activities such as ploughing, planting, weeding and harvesting. *Izinyanga* also did not perform their medical functions.

Traditionally, an alliance of chiefs and spirit mediums enforced the observance of the day. As nationalism took hold in the late fifties and early sixties, loyalty to traditional practices was considered important.

In the Nkayi and Lupane districts, the situation was confused (Ranger, 1999). Some people looked to Njelele for the rain and others to the Nevana medium in Gokwe. Njelele adherents observed Wednesday as their rest day; Nevana adherents observed Thursday. This created problems in the scheduling of meetings in the two districts. It was finally resolved that everyone south of the Shangani River should go to Njelele and north of it everyone should go to Nevana.

Anyone who broke the observance was punished. At the spiritual level an individual could have his crops destroyed by baboons or other pests. Sometimes lightning could strike his homestead. At the secular level, punishment was meted out by the chief. An individual who failed to observe a holy day could be fined an animal, such as a goat or sheep, or even a bucket of *uphoko*. Sometimes these fines were added to the *Zunde raMambo* (Tithe for the King).

"At the end of the day the chief would eat it (the fine) on behalf of the people," says Charles Maunze with a sarcastic smile.

If an individual persisted in defying the custom, he could even be evicted from the chief's area. It was feared he would bring bad omens to the rest of the people. It was religious sacrilege to plough on a *chisi* – *akarima paachisi/walima ngosuku lokuzila*. With the rise of rural nationalism, "the ideology of the cult was used to rebuke and repress the acquisitive aspirations of Christian entrepreneurs. This expressed itself mainly through a campaign to enforce the cult's rest days" (Ranger, 1999). For example Chief Bhidi Ndiweni of Matabeleland South instructed his people to observe the holy day. The wrongdoers were fined five shillings for the messenger who arrested them.

Progressive farmers were not spared the wrath of traditionalists. Mark Dokotela Ncube of northern Wenlock, in an interview with Professor

Ranger, said: "Everyone else around here believes in it. They do not farm on Wednesday and they demand that I do not. I refuse and they call me a Tshombe. I say to them, 'Stores do not close on Wednesdays; grinding mills do not close on Wednesdays. Businesses do not close. If they do, then I will close. My farm is a business! They hate me for that'"(Ranger, 1999).

One question that is not easy to answer is how the rest day came to be observed every seven days. With the exception of Paul Damasane, everybody else agreed there was no concept of the week. After the day, the next unit of time was lunar month, *inyanga/mwedzi*. If that were true, the rest day would not have come every seven days. Interestingly, the rest days don't clash with Christian rest days. Perhaps this is one of those traditions that was created as a response to colonisation as a way of matching Christian rest days.

With regard to this practice, traditional religion and Christianity have clashed seriously. The *Bantu Mirror* of December 27, 1958 carried a report about a shrine messenger who stated that Wednesdays would be observed as the day on which prayers were to be said to the gods of rain. A decision was taken at Vizhe School that villagers disobeying the command would be punished. Further, villagers were allowed to work on Sundays.

In most areas of Matabeleland South, villagers observe both Wednesday and Sundays – losing two days of economic production is disastrous, but then that has come from our heritage of two co-existing religious worlds.

THE NAMBIYA

A brief history of the Nambiya

Abridged from *A History of North-Western Zimbabwe since 400 AD*,
by Godfrey Tabona Ncube

The Nambiya were originally a breakaway group from the Rozvi State. Oral tradition indicates that they fled because their leader, Sawanga (later Hwange), had decided to set himself up as an independent ruler early in the eighteenth century. They fled north, and then west, until they entered Leya country (present day Hwange District).
The first place they settled in was called Bhale, lying between the Gwayi, Nyantuwe and Lukosi rivers. It was at Bhale that Sawanga built a hill fortress at a place called Shangano, which became the capital of his new state. Tradition also maintains that it was at Bhale that Sawanga's people first became known as Nambiya. It seems that Shangano served as the Nambiya capital for more than half a century and spanned the reigns of three successive chiefs after Sawanga's death in 1780.
The Nambiya incorporated the Leya and other smaller groups. The Kalanga dialect of the Nambiya was then imposed on the incorporated groups.
The Nambiya are believed to have moved from Shangano to the Bumbusi area in the Upper Deka valley during the reign of the fifth Hwange, whose name was Shana (1834-60). In large measure the move appears to have been dictated by the greater suitability of the wetter soils at Bumbusi for bulrush millet, sorghum and maize, which were Nambiya staples. The new capital was sited on a rocky promontory beneath two large baobab trees that still stand today. The stone-walled enclosure was about 55 metres long and two metres high and the royal dwellings were located within this complex. The masonry on the walls was a variant of the architecture of Great Zimbabwe. The Nambiya zimbabwe, like the many other madzimbabwe scattered throughout the country, is believed to have been built primarily to symbolise the wealth, prestige and authority of the ruling class. On the largest kopje, where the Nambiya chief is believed to have lived, the walls were built between the natural rocks into the steep sides of the kopje and also at the kopje, around the area where the chief's house stood. These remarkable stone structures on kopjes are spread over a wide area around the Bumbusi site and appear to indicate where senior Nambiya lived.

The skill in stone-building demonstrated by the Nambiya may indicate that they are descendents of the earlier Torwa, who are associated with stone building, rather than the later Rozwi, who merely inherited buildings at the end of the seventeenth century.

Eye-witness accounts of contemporary European observers reveal that between 1850 and 1898 the bulk of the region's population was concentrated along the Zambezi River and the lower courses of its tributaries, while the hinterland had very little or no population. Settling in the river valleys, where there were reliable water supplies all year round and fertile alluvial soils, guaranteed the people long-term cultivation and security from famine.

The second half of the nineteenth century brought considerable changes for the Nambiya. Broadly, these changes were brought about by two different factors, one resulting from the *Mfecane* and the other by the arrival of European traders and settlers. These two events radically changed the political, economic and social structure of Nambiya society.

The first traders to reach the area are thought to have been the Portuguese and their African agents, the Chikunda, who originated in Mozambique. The Portuguese purchased a large number of young men and women who were exported as slaves. This trade seriously depleted the Nambiya population and, following the abolition of the slave trade, the Nambiya began purchasing slaves back from the Portuguese in return for ivory as a means of replenishing their population.

When the *Mfecane* first reached north-western Zimbabwe in the 1840s, the Nambiya State was ruled by Hwange Lusumbami. There was a feud between Kings Mzilikazi of the Ndebele and Sebetwane of the Kololo, who were vying for the allegiance of the Tonga and for stealing Tonga cattle on the north bank of the Zambezi. King Mzilikazi apparently suspected that Lusumbami was intriguing with the Kololo and therefore Lusumbami was executed on King Mzilikazi's order in 1853 for double-dealing. This double-dealing may have generated the myth of two hearts found in Nambiya oral traditions.

The Nambiya State was characterised by ethnic diversity. Among the various ethnic groups under Hwange were many Kalanga refugees who had fled from the *Mfecane* in the south. One such small group of Kalanga refugees under Dabatu came to settle among the Nambiya near the source of the Deka River. It seems that Dabatu began trading in guns with the Portuguese to protect himself from the Ndebele. Apparently, King Mzilikazi learnt of Dabatu's activities and sent an army in April/May 1862 under Tazela to punish the Kalanga of Dabatu. Hwange Chilisa, who was Dabatu's suzerain, was implicated in this plot against the Ndebele. Dabatu was killed near the mouth of the Deka River and the Ndebele overran the lower valleys of the Gwayi and Matetsi rivers. Hundreds of people were killed and children captured. Hwange Chilisa was forced to flee across the Zambezi in about October 1862. While some of the Nambiya fled across the Zambezi River with their ruler, others remained scattered in the rough hilly country of the south of the Zambezi. Hwange Chilisa built a new village on the north bank of the Zambezi near the mouth of the Deka River, where he became an underling of the Kololo and later of the Lozi. Apparently, this flight enabled him to live long because by June 1888 he was still alive at 76 years old. Oral tradition indicates that the return of the Nambiya to the south bank in the period 1888 to 1893 was as a result of the Ndebele invasions on the north bank.

The history of land alienation in the Wankie district begins with the activities of the German geologist, Albert Giese, who heard of 'black stones that burn' while in Botswana in 1893. Following this 'discovery' of extensive deposits of high quality coal, Giese got the Mashonaland Agency to obtain a concession from the British South Africa Company over a large area of Nambiya country in 1894. Giese had to use the Mashonaland Agency to obtain the concession because BSA Company's mining terms forbade private individuals to exploit any mineral discoveries unless they floated a company. So, in 1895 Giese pegged 1036 square kilometres of southern Nambiya land that lay between the Deka and Lukosi rivers (the Bumbusi area) as coal claims, on behalf of the Mashonaland Agency. This coal concession area became the first tract of Nambiya land to be alienated to Europeans in the Wankie district.

In the late nineteenth and early twentieth centuries the majority of the Nambiya population was concentrated in the area between the Deka and Nyantuwe rivers that extended from the Bumbusi area in the south to the Zambezi valley in the north, whence the settlement extended westward to incorporate the middle and lower Matetsi valley. When the development of the Wankie coal concession began in 1903, all the Nambiya who lived within the concession area were moved east and resettled in the Lukosi and Nyantuwe areas. The construction of the railway line from Bulawayo to the Wankie coalfield in 1903 and its extension to the Victoria Falls in 1904 led to the pegging of most of the Nambiya land that surrounded the railway and its alienation to Europeans. This land was surveyed into European farms between 1904 and1909.

By the end of the first decade of the twentieth century, 45% of the Wankie district's total area had been alienated to Europeans. In 1909 the Native Commissioner recommended the removal of all the Nambiya who lived on European land to a new locality where a reserve would be established. Consequently, the Nambiya who occupied the land that surrounded the section of the railway between Dete and the upper Matetsi were removed and resettled in the Lukosi and Nyantuwe areas. As these areas were already occupied by other Nambiya removed from the coal concession area in 1903, this created overpopulation and exerted considerable pressure on the little arable land that was available in these river valleys, since most of this area is hilly and stony. What makes the removal of the Nambiya more poignant is the fact that very little of the land was put to any productive agricultural use throughout the colonial period.

In 1914 the Native Reserves Commission demarcated 317,481 acres of extremely hilly and waterless country as the Wankie Reserve. The reserve's capacity was later found to be capable of absorbing only half of the Africans who lived outside it. An agrarian crisis was thus created in the reserves because of the concentration of a large African population in the area with insufficient agricultural land. Africans who lived on unalienated land adjacent to European farms were expelled after complaints from the Wankie District Farmers' Association to the Chief Native Commission in 1920 that these Africans were starting veld fires. This, and the introduction of a rent for unalienated land, increased the scale of Nambiya movement into the reserve after 1919.

In 1924 the overcrowded situation in the Wankie Reserve and continued influx was deemed sufficiently serious to necessitate the creation of two additional reserves, A and B. Unfortunately, the land selected for the additional reserves was of very poor quality. Consequently little settlement took place in the new reserves. In 1928 the Southern Rhodesian government declared 4,000,000 acres of unalienated land in the Wankie district as the Wankie Game Reserve. The Game Reserve took up the whole southern part of the Wankie District and all the Nambiya land that had remained south of the railway between Dete and the Lukosi River. All the Nambiya who lived in this area were forcibly removed to the north of the railway in 1928 and resettled in the reserves. Oral tradition maintains that many of these Nambiya resisted resettlement from the fertile flatlands. They finally moved after their villages had been burnt down by the police.

Ega Washington Sansole recounts Nambiya history

Sitting next to me in the studio is Felix Moyo, a friend from my youth. Our eyes are on today's interviewee, Ega Washington Sansole. He is here to recount the history of the Nambiya people. Felix Moyo is first to fire a salvo of questions at the former High Court Judge, a heavily built man who speaks with a deep authoritative voice.

The Nambiya originally came from Masvingo, which they term in their language *Jimba Jemabwe*, houses of stone. From Masvingo they struck north and passed through present day Mashonaland West. They entered Tongaland and finally settled in the present day Hwange District.

The predecessors of the Nambiya were the Sileya people who spoke a Tonga dialect. The Leya people called the Nambiya 'Makaranga', a people who had a half–moon mark on their brows. Further, they carved their front teeth into a V-shape. Brands of identity.

The paramount chief of the Nambiya was Sawanga. The Ndebele people corrupted his name to Zanke. The latest corruption is Hwange. Sansole maintains he should be Wange and not Hwange. Chief Hwange was special to King Mzilikazi. It was Hwange's people who re-united King Mzilikazi's party with that of Gundwane Ndiweni, then resident in the Ncema – Insiza area.

During the arduous trek, Sawanga's pregnant daughter, Chowobata (Tshowobata), was abandoned among the Tonga. She delivered during the time of the locusts, which the Nambiya call *mhashu*. The son she gave birth to was called Pashu, a Tonga corruption of *mhashu*. He grew up speaking Tonga, although his parents were Nambiya.

Pashu ruled in the areas of Lupane and Lubimbi. Meanwhile, Sawanga trekked west until he reached the confluence of the Matetsi and Zambezi rivers. There he came into contact with the Leya and the place was called Shangano (meeting place). Knowledgeable in stone masonry, Sawanga built his own town with a stone wall perimeter. Such a stone wall was called *luswingo* (plural, *masvingo*).

Ndebele raids forced some of the Nambiya to flee across the Zambezi River. However, over a period of time, the Nambiya spread out to numerous places south of the Zambezi River. Later they occupied what came to be known as Hwange National Park, Makwandara, Detema (meaning *dekekeke ye detema* or swamps) and Kamativi.

Chief Dingani Mpala is of Leya origin. His title is Chief Nelukoba. To '*koba*' in Nambiya means to share. Nelukoba shared the land with Chief Sawanga. However, it was understood that Sawanga was the *shumba* (lion), while Nelukoba was the *shumba kaji* (the lioness). The whole area from Lambo to the Gwayi River belonged to Chief Nelukoba.

A question disturbs my peace of mind. How does a Leya chief come to have a distinctly Ndebele name? Chief Nelukoba and his son were captured by the Ndebele. The two captives lived in the Mguza area, where the son was named Dingani. When the Ndebele State was destroyed in 1893, Dingani went back to his people and assumed the chieftainship.

When Sansole recounted the history of Dingani, I immediately thought of Macheng of the Ngwato. Like Dingani, he too was captured by the Ndebele and grew up in Matabeleland. On attaining the age of majority, he went back to take over the Ngwato chieftainship. His Ndebele style of government did not go down well with the Ngwato.

Succession among the Nambiya is interesting. Royal houses, *matongo*, are led by the senior elders, *makurukota*. When the reigning Hwange dies, leaders of the various *matongo* come together to choose the next house to rule. The leader so chosen could be a *muzukuru* (nephew). Chieftainship moves among the various *matongo*. It never moves from the Hwange to his son. In fact, a Hwange could not produce a son.

Once off the air, Sansole reveals to us why this was so. A Hwange was castrated to make sure he would not produce a son. This ensured that chieftainship was not confined to his own *dongo*, but various *matongo* took turns to produce the paramount chief.

One more thing we learn from Sansole. The old Nambiya language did not have an 'L' in its vocabulary. Instead, it had an 'R', which it lost under the influence of the Ndebele. This does not come as a surprise to me. Three months ago Jerry Zondo made a similar claim with regard to the Kalanga language. Perhaps true but difficult to believe!

THE VENDA

The Venda are found in South Africa's Limpopo Province and in south-eastern Zimbabwe. They, like the Manyika, Kalanga and Birwa of Zimbabwe, were spilt into two groups when colonial boundaries were marked. In South Africa, the Venda occupy the area north and west of the town of Makhado. Indications are that, in the past, the Venda occupied a much larger area.

Venda society incorporated peoples of various ethnic groupings. The original group may have been the Lubimbi of the Mbedzi clan. This would place them, in terms of origin, close to the Sotho and Nguni peoples. This would mean they were closely related to the Dziva-Hungwe people found in Zimbabwe by the Shona.

The Venda may have incorporated Shona elements as far back as the ninth and tenth centuries. This was the time when stone architecture emerged close to the confluence of the Limpopo and Shashi rivers. Since the relatives of the original Venda, namely the Sotho, Tswana, Nguni and Dziva-Hungwe, did not practise stone architecture, it would seem to suggest that it was the Shona elements that imparted stone masonry to the Venda.

More Shona groups joined the Venda, especially after the demise of the Zimbabwe State between 1450 and 1500. These immigrants were responsible for the construction of the stone buildings at Thulamela. This contact, probably the second between the Shona and Venda, accounts for similarities in the visual arts of the two groups.

The Shona who went south following the demise of the Zimbabwe State may be responsible for Venda names such as Thohoyandou. Aeneas Chigwedere (1980) suggests a similarity between Thohoyandou (head of an elephant) and the Shona *sororenzhou* (head of an elephant). The Shona who went south would have known that Murenga Sororenzhou was their ancestor. Their language was probably altered by Sotho–Tswana influences. The Sotho word for head is *thoho*.

The civil war that culminated in the creation of the Rozvi State at the close of the seventeenth century further introduced Shona immigrants into Venda society. These latest arrivals were the Singo people.

The *Mfecane* upheavals, especially the arrival of King Mzilikazi's Ndebele in Gauteng Province, forced some groups beyond the Soutpansberg to move further north. Both Venda and Birwa moved north across the Limpopo and Shashi rivers into present day Zimbabwe. Some Venda got as far as the

Matopo Hills. There were more of them in the West Nicholson – Masase areas. The Sibasa headmanship in the Insiza district of Zimbabwe is of Venda origin.

Even prior to this there had been movement up north. For example, Tumbare finally settled at Inyathi during the last quarter of the seventeenth century. He and his people had come from the land of the Thonga, which they reached in their northward migrations from Elangeni in the Mhlathuze River area.

The Malabas, who came up in the first quarter of the nineteenth century, are better known as Venda people who were closely associated with the Mwali shrine at Njelele. Apparently, there is a similar shrine in the Venda country going by the same name. If the Malabas (Shoko by totem) were part of the group which went south either at the demise of the Zimbabwe State or the inception of the Rozvi State, they would regard Murenga Sororenzou as their ancestor. That way, they would be associated with the Mwali shrine at Njelele. Only those descended from Tovera and Murenga Sororenzou could control their ancestor's shrine.

The significance of 'Amalaveni' among the Venda

When you look at his face, something strikes you immediately. The man with two long parallel marks on each of his prominent cheeks is the controversial Bulawayo based management consultant Malobele Smith Mbezi. I have come to see him to find out about his facial markings.

The people sporting these markings, who are mostly Venda or Sotho from Beitbridge and Gwanda districts of Matabeleland South, have earned themselves the nickname of *'omaleveni'*. The two pairs of the figure eleven. "These markings are not cultural markings at all. They are lasting proof of a medical practice for problematic eyes," says Mbezi emphatically. "It is not every Venda or Sotho person who sports these markings. For example, in our family of six, four of us experienced eye problems and hence have these markings. The markings are not always found on the cheeks. Some people have them above their eyebrows or in front of their ears. Red eyes are sometimes a symptom of an eye problem. To get rid of this symptom, incisions are made to bleed the ailing person."

I become more and more curious. Just how did they make the incisions and what method was used to extract the blood?

Before the advent of the razor blade, sharp stones or iron blades were used. The Venda have for a long time been a metal working people. They mined copper, which in the Venda language is called *musina*, at Musina in Limpopo Province.

The blood was sucked out by mouth in a process called *ulumeya* in Venda. The blood was then spat out. Alternatively, a horn with a hole in the narrow end was used. The bigger end was pressed against the area where an incision had been made. Air was sucked through the narrow end and some wax used to seal it. Since nature abhors a vacuum, blood was sucked into the horn called *mutungu*. These days a tennis ball cut in half is generally used in place of the mouth or horn.

Malobele Mbezi talking about this Venda medical practice reminds me of my encounter with Gogo Matshazi. She too made reference to an Ndebele medical practice of dealing with problematic eyes. The Ndebele, like the Venda, believed in bleeding such eyes. They exposed the lower eyelids, *imbedumehlwana*, and used a serated *isagogwane* leaf to scratch the inner part of the eyelids. The process is known as *ukuhahaza*.

I take advantage of my meeting with Malobele Mbezi to obtain more knowledge about the Venda. "The Venda are a multi-ethnic group. There are the original Venda, who comprise the Vhambedzi, whose totem is the crocodile, and the Ngoni, who include the Mudaus and the Dzivhanis. Venda territory stretched from Bupedi in South Africa (the Tzaneen area south-east of Polokwane) to Malugudzi Mountain, to the east of Beitbridge," says Mbezi. Luvhimbi was the chief of the Vhambedzi.

The original Venda were invaded and ruled over by the Singo at about the time of the inception of the Rozvi State. The Singo from the north of the Limpopo River were led by Dlembeu, the father of Sororenzou, who built his stone capital at Dzata near Nzhelele. Dlembeu had a big drum called *ngomalungundu*. The descendants of the Singo include Tshivihase, Mphephu, Mphaphuli, Makhado and Ramapulana, Makhado's father.

The Venda language spoken today has been influenced by Tshilebethu and Pedi among other languages. The first Shona group to invade Venda did so at the demise of the Zimbabwe State. These invaders were the Lembethu who ruled over the original Vhambedzi and Ngona.

Recent archaeological research at Thulamela in South Africa confirms the link between the Shona and the Lembethu who built Thulamela.

To bring our conversation to a close, I ask Malobele Mbezi to recount how his grandfather came to Zimbabwe. It was as a result of a war between the Afrikaners and the Venda under Makhado. The Afrikaners are said to have used canons against the Venda. Some of the Venda, under the leadership of Mphephu, fled from the Afrikaners and settled near Buhwa Mountain in the Mberengwa district. Among them were some Balemba, who possibly went to the Venda area together with Dlembeu of the Singo people. Malobele Mbezi's grandfather did not go as far as Buhwa. When the Anglo-Boer war came to a close in 1902, most of the Venda who had sought refuge in Zimbabwe returned to South Africa. However, Mbezi's parents remained behind.

Glossary

amawosana	priests of the Mwali shrine scattered all over the country who are local representatives of the Mwali deity. Amawosana, nyusa in Shona, are mostly women. It is they who send messages to Mwali and bring back responses to the people in the localities.
chidao	differentiating name among the people of the same totem. Can be seen as a subset of a totem.
Imfazo	Ndebele word for the 1893 and 1896 wars. The word implies a high number of deaths, accompanied by a lot of bloodshed.
imitha	a woman who has given birth to a baby, but is unmarried
ingqwele	woman in charge of the wedding party. The word also refers to the most senior herdboy.
inhlanzi	a woman who goes to bear children for her barren sister or aunt
inkosi	the King
intombi	a girl beyond puberty
inyanga	Ndebele for traditional doctor
izinyanga	plural for inyanga, a traditional doctor
lobola	bride price, usually in the form of cattle
mbanje	marijuana
mutupo	totem, usually an animal or sea creature, for example Dube, Hove, Mhofu, Ntini.
n'anga	Shona word for traditional doctor
nkwite	one of the praises of the Dube people, used to show affection and love.
ukucola	ritual cleansing. To wish well or to accept.
ukumekeza	the bridal dance performed by a virgin bride
umcolo	the process of blessing, cleansing or purifying
umthakathi	witch or wizard
umthimba	bridal party
umuthi	medicine
umuzi	village

Bibliography

Alexander, J., McGregor, J. and Ranger, T., *Violence and Memory: One Hundred Years in the 'Dark Forests' of Matabeleland*, James Curry, Oxford, 2000

Beach, D.N., *The Shona and Zimbabwe, 900-1500*, Mambo Press, Gweru, 1980

Beach, D.N., in Dewry, W.J. and Palmenear, E.D. (editors), *Legacies of Stone: Zimbabwe Past and Present, Volume 1*, Royal Museum of Central Africa, Tervaren, 1997

Bourdillion, M.F.C., *The Shona Peoples*, Mambo Press, Gweru, 1976

Bryant, A.T., *Olden Times in Zululand and Natal*, Longmans, London, 1929

Chigwedere, A.S., *From Mutapa to Rhodes*, Macmillan, London, 1980

Cobbing, J., *The Ndebele Under The Khumalos, 1820-1896*, PhD thesis, University of Lancaster, 1976

Godwin, P., *Mukiwa, A White Boy in Africa*, Macmillan, London, 1996

Huffman, T.N. and Vogel, J.C., *The Chronology of Great Zimbabwe*, 1991

Krige, E.J., *The Social System of the Zulus,* Shuter and Shooter, Pietermaritzburg, 1977

Mahlangu P.S., *Umthwakazi*, Longman, Salisbury, 1957

Matenga, E., in Dewry, W.J. and Palmenear, E.D. (editors), *Legacies of Stone: Zimbabwe Past and Present, Volume 1*, Royal Museum of Central Africa, Tervaren, 1997

Mbiti, J.S., *African Religions and Philosophy*, Heinemann, London, 1969

Mbiti, J.S., *Introduction to African Religion*, Heinemann, London, 1991

Ncube, G.T., *A History of North-Western Zimbabwe, 1850-1960*, Mond Books. Kadoma, 2004

Nyathi, P., *Migration, Incorporation and Identity: The Case of the Bhebhe People of Zimbabwe*, unpublished

Nyathi, P., *Igugu likaMthwakazi, Imbali yamaNdebele, 1820-1893*, Mambo Press, Gweru, 1994

Nyathi, P., *Madoda Lolani Incukuthu*, Mambo Press, Gweru, 1999

Nyathi, P., *Lawo Magagu: Material Culture of the AmaNdebele*, Reach Out, Pietermaritzburg, 2000

Nyathi, P., *Alvord Mabena, The Man and His Roots*, Priority Projects, Harare, 2000

Nyathi, P., *Traditional Ceremonies of AmaNdebele*, Mambo Press, Gweru, 2001

Posselt, F.W.T., *Fact and Fiction*, Bulawayo, 1935

Pwiti, G., in Dewry, W.J. and Palmenear, E.D. (editors), *Legacies of Stone: Zimbabwe Past and Present, Volume 1*, Royal Museum of Central Africa, Tervaren, 1997

Ramose, M.B., in Beach D.N., *The Shona and Zimbabwe, 900-1500*, Mambo Press, Gweru, 1980

Ranger, T., *Voices from the Rocks*, James Curry, Oxford, 1999

Rasmussen, R.K. and Rubert S.C., *Historical Dictionary of Zimbabwe*, The Scarecrow Press, London, 1990

Reynolds, P. and Cousins, C.C., *Lwaano Lwanyika, Tonga Book of the Earth*, Panos, London, 1993

Thomas, C.C., *Thomas Morgan Thomas, Pioneer Missionary 1828-1884*, undated

Thomas M.T., *Eleven Years in Central Southern Africa*, Books of Rhodesia, Bulawayo, 1970

Wentzel, P.J., *Nau Dzaba Kalanga, Volume 1: Texts and Translations; Recorded by Masola Kumile*, University of South Africa, Pretoria, 1983